WRITE THAT DOWN!
THE COMEDY OF MALE ACTRESS
CHARLES PIERCE

by
Kirk Frederick

Foreword by
Armistead Maupin

Havenhurst Books
Los Angeles

Havenhurst Books

Published by Havenhurst Books, Los Angeles, CA 90046
Edited by Chris Freeman

Cover and chapter design by Jaime Flores. Book layout by the author.

This is a work of nonfiction. All names used are real and actual, and, where needed or appropriate, permission has been granted to include them. Quotations of lyrics and reviews are as originally written, and, where appropriate, permission has been granted to use them.

Library of Congress Cataloging-in-Publication Data applied for by publisher.

ISBN #s 0-9822853-8-8 and 978-0-9822853-8-1

First Edition

Charles as Bette Davis

Charles Pierce
1926-1999

Charles Pierce as Bette Davis, and as himself. Montage by Charles Pierce, 1985

WRITE THAT DOWN!
THE COMEDY OF MALE ACTRESS
CHARLES PIERCE

TABLE OF CONTENTS

For Michael

who shares my admiration and appreciation of Charles,
and whose patience and sense of humor helped
get me through writing all this down.

Charles as "Celene Kendall" (his *nom de drag*) at Ciro's in Los Angeles, 1971

"He who laughs, lasts."
– Mary Pettibone Poole, from "Beggars Can't Be Losers,"
A Glass Eye at a Keyhole, 1938

FOREWORD

by Armistead Maupin

n 1971, when I was fresh out of the Navy, a couple of friends took me out on the town in San Francisco. We ended up in a nightclub called Gold Street in an alley of the same name on what was once the Barbary Coast. The place struck me then as something out of "Have Gun, Will Travel," a TV western that had shaped my early impression of Old San Francisco. There was a mirror-backed bar and a long mezzanine from which a curving staircase descended dramatically. That's where I first saw Charles Pierce make an entrance, lingering on that staircase, blowing kisses to the crowd below as he milked every drop of their adoration.

As strange as it seems now, this was my first experience of a female impersonator – or a "Male Actress," as Pierce preferred to call himself. My feeling in that moment was one of exhilaration and mild anxiety. I was 27 years old and had only recently joined the ranks of men-loving men. I was worried, frankly, that I had just passed the point of no return, that I might be permanently altered by my first sight of a man in off-the-shoulder black satin. I was right about that.

Something in me broke that night; some tightly coiled mechanism I had carried since puberty was finally released through laughter. When Charles strode across that stage, alternately swiveling and smoking as Bette Davis, or bellowing at the balcony as Tallulah Bankhead, it was blazingly clear that being gay was not just okay but a helluva lot of fun. The jokes were often corny and vulgar, the posturing bitchy, but there was something behind those huge rolling blue eyes that spoke of great kindness and intelligence. The audience, including me, wanted him to stay there all night. His presence felt like a benediction from some mad, marauding angel.

Charles Pierce as himself, relaxing after a show at Gold Street, 1971

It's tiresome to say that you had to have been there, but you did. If you didn't catch Pierce in intimate venues like Gold Street or the Venetian Room or long-gone clubs in Manhattan like The Village Gate and Freddy's Supper Club, you can't fully understand the power of his gift. He did cameos in sitcoms in the '70s and '80s whenever a man in a dress was required, but they weren't that funny. You'll find him in the dressing room and as emcee in the 1988 film of Harvey Fierstein's *Torch Song Trilogy*, though the feeling there is more like a walk-on from a beloved elder statesman. There are YouTube videos of Pierce's 1982 appearance at the Dorothy Chandler Pavilion in Los Angeles, where he seemed to be performing in an airplane hangar, so his act, to my mind, suffered accordingly.

These days if you invoke Charles Pierce to people under fifty, they are likely (if they even recognize the name) to confuse him with the other legendary Charleses-in-drag – Charles Ludlam and Charles Busch. A younger friend of mine was certain he had seen Charles Pierce as a regular on TV's "Match Game" until we established that he was thinking of Charles Nelson Reilly. It's wonderful, therefore, to see that someone has emerged to remember and preserve Pierce's singular legacy for people who never got to experience him in person. What I remember, beyond all that healing laughter, was a dream he implanted in me on that first night at Gold Street.

When the show was over and Pierce was taking his bow, he brought out his stage managers to share in the applause. They were two gorgeous young men about my age – a blond named Kirk and a brunette named Peter – and, according to their doting boss, they were celebrating their second anniversary that November night. Even the straight folks in the audience went wild, and I was instantly filled with the hope that such an openly shared romance might truly be possible for me. How could I have guessed that I would eventually become friends with these men, or that one of them – the blond one – would one day write the book you are holding in your hands?

–Armistead Maupin
San Francisco
August 2015

Charles Pierce as himself in New York, 1985, in a portrait by Kenn Duncan

CHAPTER 1

INTRODUCTION

From the beginnings of his career as a self-proclaimed "stand-up comic in a dress," Charles Pierce, a.k.a. "**Male Actress**" and "Grand Impostor of iconic Hollywood celebrities," ad-libbed a lot.

In 1954, after he had graduated as an actor from the Pasadena Playhouse but found little stage work, Charles started playing small nightclubs. He perfected a comedy act for 15 years, doing impressions of movie stars, performing mostly pre-recorded pantomime shows, campy, gay-themed skits, plus song-and-dance routines. He opened and closed his shows with live material, most of which he wrote himself, and much of which he invented impromptu on stage.

His uncanny ability to create new material on the spot grew as fast as his audiences, so by the time we met and I began working as his stage manager in 1969, I would hear "**Write that down!**" from Charles on stage quite often, after a spontaneous new line had generated raucous audience response. All I heard was the response.

[**Bold** type is used throughout to indicate CP lines and quotes.]

Most of the time I was distracted backstage, so the task of writing down specifics of new material fell to the light and sound booth staff. Even they sometimes failed to remember an ad-lib verbatim, so we started videotaping (a new technology in the early '70s) every performance. Occasionally I would write things down, but now we also had a permanent record of Charles's comedy material on tape.

Charles worked for six consecutive years (1963–1969) at San Francisco's Gilded Cage nightclub, where he became a local celebrity as word got out about his unique comedy act. Even legendary *San Francisco Chronicle* columnist Herb Caen mentioned him almost weekly, quoting a new *bon mot* Charles had come up with, which audience members (or Charles) would call in to Herb's office. Eventually Charles's impressions of stars like Bette Davis became full routines. By 1965, he finally decided to go into full drag on stage at "The Cage."

After his Gilded Cage run came to an end in June 1969, Charles performed on weekends through that summer at the Fantasy, a little end-of-the-alley downtown nightclub. A block up Mason Street, the off-Broadway hit show *Geese* had just opened to glowing reviews and sold-out audiences at the intimate Encore Theatre, former San Francisco home to the Actors Workshop "black box" studio space in the basement below the Stage Door movie theatre.

To celebrate the successful summer run of this ahead-of-its-time two-act play about two young gay couples, the original New York producers of *Geese*, Phil Oesterman and Jim Sink, took the entire San Francisco cast and crew of the show to the Fantasy to share this "un-freaking-believably funny comic" they had discovered the weekend before.

It was the first time I had ever seen Charles. Shortly after I moved to San Francisco in May 1969, a friend who had seen and loved Charles at The Gilded Cage took me to see his show there on a busy Saturday night, close to the end of his six-year run. We got as far as the club's front bar, but could not get anywhere near the oversold showroom in back. All we heard was the roar of laughter and applause coming from the crowd through the curtain that separated the two rooms.

So there I was at the Fantasy club a few months later, with the rest of the *Geese* company that I was now part of (as the show's house manager and understudy), enjoying Charles and his clever, witty material, delivered by this attractive man doing unique impressions – parodies really – of 20th century screen queens. For me it was "like-at-first-sight," later turning to awe backstage when we all met this quite manly, animated, charming presence in person, out of drag.

During his opening monologue that night, when he chatted informally with the audience, Charles asked someone where he was from.

When he replied, "Hayward" (then a sleepy bedroom community along the southeast shore of San Francisco Bay), Charles snapped back: **"If they ever give the United States an enema, the tube goes in Hayward: the only hole above ground."** One didn't often hear that kind of material, certainly not in the late '60s. We all howled throughout his hysteria-inducing show.

His impressions were extraordinarily original, coupled with his ease as an entertainer, his elegance as a lady on stage, and his perfect timing as a comedian. My favorite, most memorable line of the night, **"I'm really very masculine; I dress this way to counteract it,"** was delivered in a mellifluous baritone voice coming from a well made-up, wigged, and glamorously dressed Hollywood blonde bombshell.

A month later, Charles became part of the cast in *Geese*. The show had run almost six months, and when audience numbers lagged in the fall, producers Phil and Jim decided to "celebrity cast" Charles Pierce.

Geese was a sweet, touching play that dealt with the subject of homosexuality at a time when parents were searching for answers to their children's coming out. Act One was about a young girl in Texas bringing her college "girlfriend" home for the holidays to confused, unwelcoming parents, and a spinster aunt who discovers the girls are lesbians.

Act Two began with 'Little' Bill (as his parents called him), an attractive 18-year-old collegian, coming into his mom and dad's bedroom to say that he was off to the frat house for a "rush" party. His mother Helen and father Bill Sr. continued their "George and Martha"-inspired scenes (catty, à la *Who's Afraid of Virginia Woolf?*) on one side of the stage, while their gay son Bill and his new frat friend Hank carried on their tender getting-to-know-you scenes in Bill's bedroom on the other side.

Charles as Helen (center) in *Geese*, 1969, with Paul Shumacher, Kirk (left) and Peter

It helped ticket sales that by the end of both of the girls' and boys' first scenes in their bedrooms, they had slowly stripped off their clothes and were completely naked, making – then gradually falling in – love. Audiences embraced the sweet stories, with four young performers having convincingly staged and cleverly lighted simulated same-sex. (*Hair* was playing across the street at the Geary Theatre; it was getting all the attention about on-stage nudity. Our performances were professional and tasteful. The love-making seemed natural. No one bothered us.)

For four months after *Geese's* successful San Francisco summer opening, the domineering mother of Little Bill had been played by a strong actress who needed to leave the show in the fall, so Phil and Jim came up with the idea to cast Charles as Little Bill's mother. They also cast the famed topless performer Carol Doda as the girlfriend in Act One. New casting, more publicity, and good reviews helped; the show ran for another year.

Charles got raves for his performance as the mother. He also got thanks and gratitude from everyone in the show, and from the appreciative audiences, for playing it straight, not "camping it up" and distracting from the play's simple and supportive message that it was acceptable for two young adults of the same sex to fall in love. Again, this was 1969!

What attracted Charles to the part of Helen in *Geese* was the writing. In the scenes with her husband, Charles-as-Helen would breathe new life into the well-wrought words of playwright Gus Weill. His Helen was a smart but sassy, savvy but bitchy, loving but controlling wife, and the approving mother of a gay son. Modern theatre hadn't seen a character like this. Charles was honored to play her, and to be acting again, even if it was as a woman. (This was when he first invented his "**Male Actress**" moniker; in the Shakespearean tradition, he had trained as an actor who could play women as easily and convincingly as men.)

Charles had written his own comedy material for almost 20 years; he knew how to craft dialogue. And monologue. *Geese* taught him even more, and he spent his days writing new lines for his own nightclub act. In the spring of 1970, he and the *Geese* producers decided to try out his newly created show he called *Charles Pierce and His Boys,* which premiered at the Encore Theatre on "Cabaret Mondays," *Geese's* one "dark" night of its performance week.

Charles Pierce and His Boys became an instant hit. Peter Still and I ("His Boys") performed various skits and dance routines with Charles, one

Charles Pierce and His Boys, Kirk (left) and Peter, 1970

of our most popular being a pantomimed, fully staged dance performance of a number from the new off-Broadway show *Dames at Sea* (above).

Peter and I had met playing Little Bill and Hank in *Geese,* and became a couple for the next eight years. We also became Charles's stage managers and dressers; he called us his show's "Production Coordinators." Working backstage throughout most of the show, Peter and I prepared for Charles's next costume change, called light and sound cues, pre-set or took props on stage as requested, and made sure the show ran smoothly.

Charles wrote most of his own nightclub act over the years. Fans or friends gave him lines, writers would sell him jokes ("**I never paid more than $5 a line,**" he would boast), and even his mother Jessie contributed some material. But he worked almost every day of his professional life on the act, taking out anything that wasn't working, writing something new, concocting different costumes or props, or creating witty lines for his ladies to say. And the man had such a gift for improvisation, he ad-libbed hysterically funny things during almost every show. It became one of my main tasks over the 20+ years we worked together to "**write that down**."

: : : : :

After Charles died in 1999, I unearthed my collection of sketchy notes about his material, program biographies, press releases announcing various performance engagements, newspaper reviews, scores of publicity photographs over the years, and, most importantly, those old, grainy black-and-white videotapes we had recorded of his shows starting in the early '70s. Luckily, I also gained access to the two major archives of his papers.

After many old fans and friends encouraged me for years to write the book about Charles, I finally decided to write down as much of his shows' brilliant comedy material as I could find and recall, which partly involved digitizing and transcribing his shows from those old videotapes. There are a few memories and observations of my own just to add perspective, but this is all about his material.

The book is structured as Charles constructed his shows, in segments about his primary characters: the Hollywood Blondes (Carol Channing, Marlene Dietrich, Marilyn Monroe, Barbara Stanwyck), Mae West, Katharine Hepburn, Joan Collins, Bette Davis and her various nemeses including Tallulah Bankhead and Joan Crawford, then his Finales, the Applause, rave Reviews, and a final chapter about some carryings-on After the Show.

His comedy material is compiled in approximately the order it was delivered during a typical nightclub performance, including somewhat chronologically compiled routines from early 1970s shows through his last appearance in 1994. He perfected the delivery of his material over the years, so some of the early lines may have changed gradually, usually for the better. Occasionally lines and jokes are included as they originated from his numerous spontaneous ad-libs.

The primary reason for my writing this down is to share his witty stand-up comedy material, plus a few anecdotes, as well as some visual reminders – mostly questionable-quality black-and-white publicity photos – of the popular, versatile entertainer. This is not a complete biography nor historical overview, not a tell-all book about offstage antics, not a sleazy look at a performer's sordid life. His wasn't. Charles was a regular guy, with no scandal, no nasty quirks, no ugly tragic persona lurking behind a mask of comedy. He was a gifted and giving performer, an inspired writer, a generous employer, and a great friend, as well as a clever, insightful, talented impressionist of legendary Hollywood stars, mostly female.

: : : : :

Charles was diagnosed with prostate cancer in early 1997. He and I had worked together off and on from 1969 through 1990, when he retired and I started a new career in the cruise industry. Our lives went in separate directions, his into retirement, mine into sailing the world.

Two years after his diagnosis, in late May of 1999, his bosom buddy Bea Arthur called to tell me Charles was dying. I was out on the high seas and did not get her message till I returned home June 2. When I opened that morning's *Los Angeles Times*, the large obituary headline read "Charles Pierce; Actor Impersonated Female Stars." He had died in his sleep two nights before, on Monday, May 31, Memorial Day. He was 73, it said. Actually, he would have been 73 in another six weeks, on July 14.

"Pierce," it continued, "who repeatedly announced his retirement during the 1980s, died Monday at his home in Toluca Lake."

How glamorous, I thought. It was actually North Hollywood, although Charles often called it "Toluca Lake Adjacent." (The town of Toluca Lake was fancier; Bob Hope and other big stars lived there.)

The obit's opening sentence began with "Charles Pierce, a female impersonator…" A few paragraphs later it quoted Charles as having said during a 1988 interview in the same paper, **"Why do I always have to be described as 'Charles Pierce, female impersonator'? Why not just 'Charles Pierce, actor'?"**

Other obituaries appeared in major urban newspapers over the next few days. *The New York Times* also started its obit with the "fem imp" tag, but duly noted that Charles was "a pioneer in the form, [and] set the stage for a future generation of impersonators, but preferred to be known as an actor rather than a 'drag queen.' No one who was anyone escaped inclusion in his vast repertory of leading ladies whom he wickedly caricatured 'with slashing histrionic flashes of insight,' said Clive Barnes in *The New York Times*, reviewing Mr. Pierce's first New York performance [at The Village Gate] in 1975."

San Francisco Chronicle theatre critic Steven Winn wrote his newspaper's obit, also quoting Charles: "**I'm really just an actor who puts on certain costumes, generally gowns, to create female characters familiar to millions of people.**"

Mr. Winn also noted that "the gay audience loved him. So did suburban housewives and anyone else who saw how deeply funny a man in a dress, dishing Hollywood stardom, could be."

"An Appreciation" of Charles that his friend, actor/writer Michael Kearns, wrote for the *Los Angeles Times* a few days later cleverly observed that "playing a woman who impersonated movie stars afforded Charles the opportunity to be more of himself. Their vulnerability, their bitchery, their vanity and their brutality were extensions of his authentic self. Perhaps that's why, even though he was clearly a man's version of a woman, it was never a condescending lampoon. He respected these women."

In their remembrances of celebrities who had died in 1999, both *LIFE* and the *Sunday New York Times Magazine* included large photos and lengthy blurbs about Charles in their January 2000 retrospective issues. In its *LIFE* REMEMBERS section, the publication's "Year in Pictures" included Joe DiMaggio, Mel Tormé, George C. Scott, Sylvia Sidney, Stanley Kubrick, Wilt Chamberlain, Dusty Springfield, John Erlichman, Señor Wences, John F. Kennedy Jr., and Charles Pierce ("the doyen of drag"). It was impressive company, and impressive that Charles was included among them.

Under two large photos of Charles as Norma Desmond and as himself, the *Sunday New York Times Magazine* writer Thomas Mallon subtitled his "Crossing" article, "He dressed up Jack Benny's comic timing in Mae West's clothes," and began by quoting one of Charles's typical responses to an audience member: "**Of course I'm too much! If I were too little, I wouldn't be up here!**"

Mr. Mallon also pointed out that long after Charles's death, drag had proved resilient, even mainstream: "Lypsinka performs in clubs as Charles Pierce's most accomplished heir, kids tune in to RuPaul on TV, and politicians hustle for votes at Wigstock." Mallon quipped that Charles's ashes now reside at Forest Lawn – a short distance from Bette Davis – and his lithe spirit is strutting, as he put it, "one high-heeled step beyond."

Several hundred of Charles's closest and most intimate friends and fans gathered on June 19, 1999, at Forest Lawn, for what emcee Michael Kearns announced was "The Last Charles Pierce Show."

While attending his funeral service, I flashed back to early 1995, when Charles had called my partner Michael Laughlin and me to welcome us back to Los Angeles (we had just returned from working in Florida for a year), and to say he would like to invite us on his personally conducted "Graveline Tour" of Forest Lawn.

We three walked through burial sites of the stars, while Charles entertained us with funny stories such as Bette Davis being entombed at the cemetery entrance on the hill above Warner Brothers' Burbank studio; from here, Charles said, "**she could look down on Jack Warner for eternity**." We three may have had a few too many laughs, if the glaring gazes of cemetery volunteers were any indication.

On the opposite side of the Forest Lawn entrance was the equally monumental sarcophagus of Charles's old friend Liberace, entombed alongside his brother and mother. Charles suggested that all their crypts had Liberace music piped into them, also for eternity. True? Why not?

We walked back to the spacious Columbarium of Radiant Dawn, where a small door engraved "Morton" was the only sign of Lucille Ball's urn (since moved). Then Charles marched us around the corner to the Columbarium of Providence, where he proudly announced he had just purchased a space there for $100,000, and planned an elaborate site for his urn, complete with a brass plaque of his face.

After that hysterically funny, oddly informative, and most unforgettable day, Charles and I were not in touch much again except for birthday celebrations, catch-up dinners at local gay restaurants (including the Venture Inn, always in the center booth under a large poster of Charles as Bette Davis), and occasional visits to theatre or comedy shows. The cancer prompted his withdrawal into seclusion, and after the diagnosis, Charles spent weeks, perhaps months, creating and writing his own funeral service, and assembling his vast collection of memorabilia for archiving.

Michael Kearns hosted the service and first greeted the 400+ Forest Lawn guests by reading Charles's own words of praise for his long-time friend Donald Lee Kobus, who took care of him during his last few months. Don said that Charles was "not a drag queen; he was a control queen." He had planned every detail of his funeral, which he wanted to be enjoyed as a "show," complete with laughter. Charles even quoted the old adage, "He longest laughs who laughs the last."

Forest Lawn's Church of the Hills was packed with old friends and avid fans: Bea Arthur. Carole Cook. Rip Taylor. Alice Ghostley. Actor pals Conrad Bain, Bill Erwin, Michael Jeter, and Mary Jo Catlett. Shirley Temple's son Charlie Black. Long-time Charles Pierce show pianists Joan Edgar and Peter Mintun. Cabaret legends Sharon McNight and Shelley Werk. Franklin Townsend, the stylist who first got Charles into full "drag." Comic impressionist Michael Greer.

As my partner Michael Laughlin said, we were the only ones there that we had never heard of. ("**Write that down**," I could almost hear Charles urging from his urn.)

Bea Arthur told a favorite gay joke, then added a few touching words about her good friend. She ended her part of the funeral service by singing Noël Coward's "I'll See You Again," accompanied simply and elegantly by Lori Andrews on the harp.

> *I'll see you again whenever spring breaks through again…*
> *This sweet memory across the years will come to me.*
> *Though my world may go awry*
> *In my heart will ever lie*
> *Just the echo of a sigh.*
> *Good-bye.*

There was not a dry eye in the church. But there was thunderous applause; it was perhaps the longest ovation the man (or Bea) ever got. Charles had asked Michael Kearns to read one last poem:

> *A man may kiss a maid good-bye.*
> *The sun may kiss a butterfly.*
> *The morning dew may kiss the grass.*
> *And you, my friends [pause]… farewell.*

That was so typical of Charles: getting the last laugh, and perhaps a little dig at some friends who had fallen out of touch during his retirement and illness.

And as someone else said, I think it was actor and longtime friend Elliot "Ted" Reid, Charles would have been thrilled with this sold-out house. Just think, Ted suggested, of how much Charles would have made had there been a cover charge! Charles would have loved that. He was Scottish. And proud of it.

He also would have loved the laughter and the applause. He was a performer. And a damn good one. He was certainly the funniest stand-up comic in a dress I ever knew, heard of, or saw.

This is Charles Pierce's story – mostly about his last 20 years as a nightclub performer, and especially about his comedy material – reported by the guy who worked as his stage manager, dresser, production coordinator, occasional producer, director, manager, publicist, co-performer, devoted friend, and admirer from 1969 to 1990: over twenty years of mirth and merriment. And good times.

I'm often asked why Charles didn't write his own book. The truth is, I don't know. Maybe he just procrastinated, then ran out of time. As early as 1981, he was quoted as saying that someday he would write an autobiography called "From Drags to Riches."

He did start a book he called "**No Title Yet** by Charles Pierce, *The Story of My Lives: Confessions of a Male Actress*," but it was only about his early life, up to his years at The Gilded Cage in the 1960s. He never finished it. Notes and excerpts from the memoir that he had started are included in this book's Appendix, plus another piece he wrote called "Charles Pierce Interviews Charles Pierce."

It's taken awhile for me to "write that down," but here it is, at last. Enjoy the laughs. Charles was the master – and mistress – of laughter.

Ladies and gentlemen, introducing Mister Charles Pierce.

Charles Pierce,
Bea Arthur,
Kirk Frederick,
1993

Charles as his "generic Hollywood blonde," looking here like Carol Channing

CHAPTER 2

THE BLONDES THAT HOLLYWOOD FORGOT

"**N**o, no, no,**"** he pouted, stomping his fashionable high-heeled pump. **"I'm not a female impersonator. And I'm certainly not a drag queen. I'm a Male Actress!"**

This Charles Pierce signature line from his irrepressible 1970s and '80s comedy act summed up the attitude he had developed about his own career path and chosen profession.

After graduating from the Pasadena Playhouse school of acting in the late '40s, he soon realized there was a dearth of paying jobs for actors, especially comedic ones. Charles started working small comedy clubs from Altadena, California, to Miami, Florida, in the early '50s, perfecting his unparalleled ability to invent and share comic impersonations of famous Hollywood stars, and provide wickedly funny material for them to say.

His were more impressions than impersonations. His supple, almost gender-neutral face took on a particular look of the celebrity. He would adjust his vocal intonation and inflection to match the star's, and his quick wit provided clever words to capture the essence of the character with a funny, finely tuned one-liner. He was a rare combination of talents.

The man's comic timing was flawless, matched by his improvisational acting ability to mimic the person instantly and accurately. His keen writing helped, and eventually, so did complete costumes, female makeup, and appropriate wigs.

But what distinguished this unique genius was his knack for capturing the essence of a character with his eyes: large, expressive, piercingly blue.

One particularly original and explosively funny routine started as an ad-lib he invented during a show he did shortly after actress Joan Crawford died in 1977. As Bette Davis, who famously hated Ms. Crawford, Charles bugged his big, Bette Davis eyes, pursed his lips, twirled his arms, flicked a cigarette, and withered the audience with the cutting:

"So Joan Crawford's dead." [*Dead* is pronounced, in Charles's truly abrupt Bette Davis style, *tet*. He would pause, flick cigarette ashes, turn his head slightly and say sweetly:]
"Now, we must speak good of the dead." [Pause. Flick ashes again. With faux sadness:]
"And Joan's dead." [Pause.]
"Good." [Pronounced like *could*, ending with a 't']

Long before the mid-'60s when Charles got into full glamour drag to open or close his act at The Gilded Cage, he had worked many small clubs across the country where it was then illegal to cross-dress on stage (especially in certain states like Florida during the 1950s). He appeared in a dark suit or tuxedo, often with a cape or other non-specific piece of character wardrobe like an apron or shawl, with a box of props at hand.

A cigarette holder, a funny hat or turban, a feather boa, a leopard stole, or a frumpy dime-store wig helped establish the character he was playing. Then-popular pre-recorded "record pantomimes" became the mainstay of his shows, but he would open and close the evening with his own live material, often extemporaneously.

Impressions of Charles Laughton and Jack Benny were tossed off, along with moments of '30s and '40s First Lady Eleanor Roosevelt (actually his very first impression on stage) or Mae West. Usually in one phrase, the character was established, often without introduction or explanation.

With a shawl, a curly gray wig, and a mink stole with alligator clip "mouths," he would assume a sing-song voice, and blurt out: **"Franklin, get out of the water. You'll catch your death of polio!"** Audiences in the 1950s and '60s instantly knew it was Eleanor Roosevelt.

Eleanor's relationship with Lorena Hickok prompted a Charles-as-Eleanor ad-lib early in his career: **"Franklin, if you can have a mistress, then so can I! Lorena asked to see the inside of a Washington monument, so I let her."**

Charles as Eleanor Roosevelt, c. 1950s (left) and 1970s (right)

Then Charles-as-Eleanor held up the fur stole heads, introducing: **"Flora and Fauna: this one speaks; the other does not."**

Eleanor continued by announcing that she was on her way to Manila, **"to congratulate the people there on their envelopes."**

Charles rarely got political; he left that to the Mort Sahls of his day. But every four years as election hysteria increased, Charles said that if HE ran and won, **"You would not only get a President, you'd save a salary by getting a First Lady, too."**

During the Vietnam War, Charles suggested how guys could beat the draft. **"Very simple. You walk into your draft board as Bette Davis, twirl your arms, purse your lips, and in your very best Davis drawl, ask, 'Now what's all this crap about Veet-nam?'"**

::::::

Many mid-century film and television personalities were larger than life, and their facial expressions or vocal idiosyncrasies were ideal fodder for Charles's comedy impressions. As the years and his shows went on, it was the famous female Hollywood icons that became his favorite "targets." Eventually, they would be costumed and wigged appropriately.

A typical Charles Pierce show in the '70s and '80s would open with impressions of The Blondes: Carol Channing, Marlene Dietrich, Marilyn Monroe, and Barbara Stanwyck, all done in a generic glamour gown and a basic blonde wig.

Mae West would show up later in full regalia, in her own segment. His Katharine Hepburn would usually be casually attired in black slacks and a turtle neck, or a coolie jacket, or a nun's whipple, cape, and disheveled gray wig, recalling Kate as Eleanor of Aquitaine from *The Lion in Winter*.

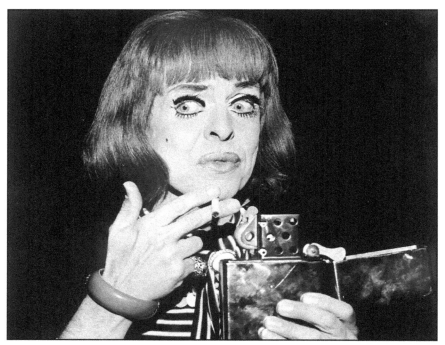

Charles as Bette Davis, c. 1975

Probably his best and always popular impression was Bette Davis. As one of the most well-known stars he "did," Bette was also his broadest. He exaggerated her famed idiosyncrasies (pursed lips, bugged eyes, twirling arms, wide-legged walk, perennial cigarette in hand) for comic effect and it worked. This was his most campy, over-the-top impression.

The Charles-as-Bette bitch fights (or "cat fights" as they were then called by the media that could not use the word *bitch*) were carried on with the likes of Joan Crawford and Tallulah Bankhead. Charles-as-Bette would change only his expression (usually just his eyes: bugged, squinting, or frowning) and his voice to achieve uncanny, instantaneous impressions of her nemeses and sparring victims.

Bette always won. (And she gets her own chapter later, to show why.)

In the early half of the 20+ years that we worked together, mostly in San Francisco, Charles ended his show by performing the only fully (some say over-) staged and costumed, lip-synced pantomime production number he retained from his shows' earlier years: to Jeanette MacDonald's recorded "San Francisco" from the famed earthquake movie.

As he played more cities where fewer fans knew about Jeanette or San Francisco or "San Francisco," and when he performed at larger venues like the opulent Venetian Room of the Fairmont Hotel on San Francisco's Nob Hill (where the ceilings

Charles as Jeanette MacDonald, c. 1971

were too high for the number's long, trapeze-like swing), the routine was dropped, and his Bette Davis segment ended the show.

Later, he added a final glamour outfit for the closing segment, sang a farewell song or two, did several more ad-libbed final lines (depending on the crowd), flipped the wig around or dragged out yet another feather boa, and carried on until he knew exactly when to leave the audiences screaming for more.

Fewer and fewer male celebrities were included in his routines. Occasionally an impression of Jack Benny would slip into Charles's full glamour-drag opening segment, usually just so he could deliver one of his favorite lines: "**Just because I'm dressed like this, doesn't mean I can't do a man.**" [Wait for it.]

"**Male Actress**" was just one of the many monikers Charles invented for himself over his 40 years of performing, from the mid-1950s into the 1990s. Once his drag persona started in the '60s, he billed himself variously as "Female Impressionist," "Comedy Illusionist," "Master and Mistress of Disguise," "The Grand Impostor," "The Blondes That Hollywood Forgot,"

"Satirist in Sequins," or "Stand-up Comic in a Dress." But he rarely used the term "Female Impersonator." And never, ever "Drag Queen."

"A drag queen is one who actually believes she can give birth."

Charles didn't. And he never appeared in costume off stage. Day to day, he dressed in male attire, never wore female makeup in public, and combed his wispy strawberry blonde hair like an office worker. He had a mellow baritone/tenor voice, did not lisp or take on any other stereotypically "gay" vocal affectations, and although he walked and moved like a dancer, he was not overly effeminate. He was decidedly gay, and occasionally slipped into "gay-speak," especially after a few martinis, but he was always a man off stage.

: : : : :

In my years as his stage manager, dresser, and security cop after his shows, I would keep backstage visitors out of view until he had removed his undergarments (dance belt, three pairs of skin-colored tights, a corset with cups for falsies) and his complete stage makeup, dried and combed his own hair, and donned a sport shirt and slacks to greet guests. He was humble and gracious, but never granted requests to "do Bette Davis" off stage. Maybe a word, or a famous line or two. But never a "performance." That's what he did for a living.

"It's just an act, you know," he would say on stage in his natural voice, dressed like a movie star at the Oscars. "**I go home every night to the wife and kids: Bruce and those goddam poodles.**"

Charles typically opened every show in a generic glamour gown ("**I don't wear women's clothes. I have my costumes designed to LOOK like women's clothes. You've seen** *Women's Wear Daily***? This is what men wear nightly.**"). His form-fitting, full-length, and usually sequined costume had a split up the side to show off his gorgeous gams, and to allow for easier movement around the stage. The wig was always blonde. The makeup was always basic. The perfume was always Shalimar.

But his expressive blue eyes and that dazzling Ipana Smile (made popular in late-'40s and early-'50s TV commercials), plus his graceful, almost choreographed glides across the stage, prompted him to admit as an actor that "**Honey, you put on a blonde wig and you can be anyone you want….**"

"**Like Marilyn Monroe.**" [striking a sexy pose and cooing in her breathy, purring sex-kitten voice] "**Oooh** [rhyming with *coo*], **I was eight before I was seven. I was married to jumpin' Joe DiMaggio who had terrible dandruff, so my girlfriend told me to give him Head and Shoulders. I said, Oooh... I don't know how to give shoulders.**"

"**Or you can be Marlene Dietrich**" [which he pronounced mimicking the legendary actress's dropped L's and R's, sounding more like *Mah-wayna Dee-twick*].

If his show was ever precisely "scripted," and as far as I know it was not (in the sense that no two were ever exactly the same), the Marlene routine would have been written down something like this:

"**Hello. I'd like to do a few numbers I did during the war. Some of them are in the audience tonight. Then a scene from my latest film,** *Bikini Widow*, **where I play the part of Annette Funicello's great granddaughter. I give my love to a young boy; he looks at it, and gives it back. This pisses me off. I threaten to show him my long, beautiful, slender, theatrical-type leg.** [He does.] **By the way, ladies: you must never break wind in your panty hose. The bubbles run down your legs and blow your shoes off.**"

Charles as Marlene Dietrich, c. 1980

Charles's version of "Mah-wayna" actually sounded more like this, in a stereotypical, exaggerated German accent, dropping the L's and R's: *Heh-woe. I'd wike to do a few numbews I did doing the wah. Some of them ah win the audience tonight. Then a scene fwom my watest fi-yum,* **Bikini Widow,** *wheah I pway the pot of Annette Funichewo's gweat gwanddottah. I give my wuv to a hung boy; he wooks at it, and gives it back. This pisses me off. I thweaten to show him my wong, bootiful, swender, theatwical-type weg.* [He does.] *By the way, wadies: you must nevah bweak wind in you panty hose. The bubbles wun down you wegs and bwoh you shoes off.*

Switching back to his own voice....

"And what about Barbara Stanwyck? Remember her in 'The Big Valley' on TV? My GOD, she was butch. She wore two jock straps for a bra. Now THAT's butch. She always sounded like this [changing to a sneering, nasal, guttural "Oh no" voice]: **In 'The Big Valley' I would say, Oh no, Audra, we cahn't lose the ranch** [pronounced *raunch*]. **Quick, take my lips and go out and milk those steers. Wait, you cahn't. My lips are caught to my teeth. Oh no.**

"So I lost the ranch... I couldn't keep my calves together."

"**Now tell me where**," Charles would interrupt, "**in Stockton, California, in the 1860s, would she find that 'Big Valley' leather slacks suit that she always wore?**"

Barbara continued. "**Remember me in *Titanic?*** [the 1953 movie] **Oh no, I don't know how to go down. I've never gone down. I cahn't. My lips are caught to my teeth. Oh no.**"

Charles would generally ad-lib variations of famous lines from Stanwyck's TV shows "The Big Valley" or "Wagon Train," or from her 1944 Oscar-nominated performance in *Double Indemnity*, always starting or ending the lines with her dismissive "**Oh no**" sneer. Barbara would often "appear" in other parts of Charles's show, commenting on something questionable that another character would say; out of nowhere Barbara's iconic sneer and "**Oh no**" would interrupt the other "ladies," who would act annoyingly surprised and usually tell her to shut up and go away.

"**Carol Channing? Well, yesh**," he would giggle, bending sideways at the waist, and doing the usual wide-eyed, faux-ditsy, slightly lispy Channing. "**Well yesh... It's me, Kee-yarol Chee-yan-ning. I'm so cutesy-pie, I could puke. I went to the zoo the other day with my friend Doris Day, and her lovely sister Doodah. That's right: Doodah Day. And Pat Boone and his sister Bab. And Eartha Kitt with her brother Tool. And Shelley Winters, who wasn't with anyone, but looked like she was. Oh my, she has really packed it on, hasn't she? In the last five years her feet haven't felt rain. She was standing on the street corner the other day, wearing a blue and white sweater and a man came along and put a letter in her mouth. And she ate it! And it was delivered! Then the cops came by and told her to break it up**.

"**Well, oh my, yesh... Kee-yaroll got side-tracked there.**

"Well yesh, you see, I was at the zoo, and we went up to the monkey cage, but there were no monkeys. So I asked the zoo-keeper where the monkeys were, and he said they were in the back, mating. So I asked him, 'if I gave them a banana, would they come out?' He said, 'Would you?'

"Well yesh, I'm a little teapot, short and stout. Here is my handle [one hand would go on his hip, indicating a handle] **and here is my spout** [spoofing Carol's ditsyness, the other hand would do the same thing]. **Oops. Here is my**

Charles as Carol Channing, Gold Street, San Francisco, 1971

handle, here is my spout [same gestures; then resigned, she would giggle and gush:] **Well shit, I'm a sugar bowl."**

That Carol Channing "routine" is verbatim from one of his first shows in 1971 at Gold Street, a favorite North Beach / Barbary Coast alley haunt of Charles – and Carol herself, where she attended his show several times – for several years in the early 1970s. Much of that Carol material lasted throughout Charles's career, with minor changes or rearrangements. For instance, Eartha Kitt's brother later became "Make-Up" rather than "Tool."

In the late '60s and early '70s, his shows' opening segments also included impressions of B-movie stars, some blonde, some not, who wore turbans in their movies. Before it was legal for men to wear women's clothes and wigs on stage, Charles would turn his back to the audience, dig into his prop box, and slide on a bejeweled turban, announcing, "**And now: the Turban Ladies.**" He turned around and asked, "**Who here remembers Maria Montez**?" After counting aloud the number of raised hands, he'd say, "**So that accounts for the six iron lungs parked outside.**"

He did a silly take-off of the Caribbean Cyclone's films: "**Every movie I ever made was called *The Cobra Jewel*,**" followed by several moments from Ms. Montez's scenes about the giving, getting, stealing, retrieving, or searching for the "cobra jewel," as if it were the Hope Diamond. "**You don't *have* the cobra jewel? Oy *and* veh, both!**" Breaking character:

Charles as Maria Montez

"**I do go way back, you know,**" he would say, apropos of nothing. "**There were two of me on the ark. I was the one with the turban and long nails.**"

With a switch in accent from Montez's faux Spanish to bad Russian, Charles introduced "**the other Maria: Maria Ouspenskaya, the gypsy lady, who wore authentic naugahyde outfits, with a lot of keys that hung down and down, and opened nothing. She and Wanda Landowska lived together for awhile, but they couldn't fit both their names on the mailbox, so they had to break up.**

"**Then the gypsy lady spoke. 'When the moon is full, and the wolfbane is in bloom, you will change.** [To a couple in the front row:] **You will become her. She will become you. No one will know the difference. You will become Transylvanian Transvestites.'**

"**Then she had the balls to sing.**" (Badly, to an old gypsy refrain:)

"**There's a story / Each gypsy loves to hear / That if your son wears golden earrings / He's a little queer.**" (She spoke:) "**You are strange, my** son. Queer, actually. But through no fault of your own. Never mind, my son. Go on: be gay!"

Some of what the "Turban Ladies" said made little sense, but these were visual gags, not verbal. (And surreal, like many of his impressions.)

The turbaned gypsy would grab the microphone stand as if it were a shepherd's staff, and walk across the stage, saying, "**She would walk Borgo Pass with an old microphone stand, because she was too cheap to buy a stick. Kiss me quick, I'm Carmen. Oh look: there's Don Juan. You know why they called him Don Juan? Because after one, he was done.**" [Wait for it.]

Charles as Gloria Swanson / Norma Desmond

"**And now, ladies and gentlemen, and others: the greatest turban-wearer of them all...**" With eyes bugged, hands clawed aside his face, and teeth clenched, he would introduce:

"**Gloria Swanson as Norma Desmond** from *Sunset Boulevard*, **'in the 49th year of my seven-day beauty plan. I'm a great star. You know what a star is, don't you? A big ball of gas.'**

"**They accused me – me, Me, ME: Norma Desmond – of killing my lover, Joe. Oh please... I didn't kill him. I shot him, then he fell in my pool and drowned. That's all. But I didn't <u>kill</u> him. Heavens!**

"**And now I'm back with you, back to make the sequel to** *Sunset Boulevard*, **to be called** [pause, confused] **uh,** *The <u>Return</u> to Sunset Boulevard*. **We'll have to work on that title. But it's going to be in 3-D, so that I can reach out from the screen into the motion picture theater and touch all my wonderful fans sitting out there in the dark.**"

(To fans in the front row:) "**Do you have any popcorn for me? A Hostess Twinkie? An Eskimo Pie? That reminds me: I was in love with an Eskimo once, but it was cold, so we had to break it off. I put it in the hands of my lawyer. He said it wouldn't stand up in court. But it did.**"

Charles suddenly started staring down someone else in the front row, lowering his face down to theirs and saying, "**Have you ever been this close to anyone wearing so much makeup before?**"

Back to Norma. "**All of you wonderful people out there in the dark. They don't come in any more for the popcorn, the chewing gum, the peanut brittle. Do you know why? No? I'll tell you why… The people who remember me can't chew, that's why.**

"**I'm ready for my close-up, Mr. DeMille, on that part of me that never wrinkled… my teeth!**

"**It's 12 midnight on Saturday, when the Art Deco people would come out. They have no other place to go now that the movie palaces have been torn down. It'll be Grauman's Chinese Theatre next. Actually I've never seen a Chinese person in the place.**

"**I'm feeling very Ima Sumac right now. That dreadful night years ago when she went into her ninth octave. Anyone here old enough to remember Ima Sumac has one big surprise every day: you wake up!**"

After the Turban Ladies, Charles would usually go back to a blonde wig and into the "basic blonde glamour gal" he had created and called Celene Kendall, his *nom de drag*. "She" would continue with more opening stand-up comedy material, usually current and mostly topical.

During one of the first overblown media blitzes that surrounded the U.S. Senate addressing the abortion issue (roundly denounced by most religious groups), Charles's beloved mother Jessie wrote one of the many jokes she contributed to his show over the years: "**The rectory housekeeper looks up from her morning paper and says, 'Father, what are we to do about this abortion bill?' [pause] 'Pay it,' he says.**"

Concurrent with the infamous flack over Anita Bryant coming out against gays in the '70s, Charles would tell one of his favorite jokes: "**How do you tell a Florida orange from a California orange? You slice them in half and put a hole in each one, then suck on it. The one that sucks back comes from California.**

"**Do you know what we all need to do about Anita Bryant? Just shut up about her. Ignore her and she'll go away. The anonymity will** drive the bitch mad!" (The gay community liked to think that it did.)

Another of his notorious Gilded Cage jokes lasted well into the 1970s, getting a laugh from those who understood it: "**The difference between meat and fish is that if you beat your fish it will die.**"

"Gay material" had been a mainstay of his act in the early years of playing mostly gay nightclubs, so when Charles started crossing over to mixed venues in the early 1970s, there were some gay-specific lines that inevitably crossed over with him. He would tone down the raunch, but if a gay reference seemed to go over a mixed audience's collective heads, as in the joke about "**Marie Antoinette was surely not the only queen in history who lost her head over a basket,**" he would usually utter "**You have to know what I'm talking about to know what I'm talking about,**" with a sly wink to those who did.

"Dated material" abounded for years. Like Royal Family jokes in the '70s: "**Oh that's awful. Every time they have sex, Princess Anne gets a cube of sugar.**" Or old lines like "**How many actresses does it take to screw in a light bulb? Fifty: one to climb the ladder and do it, and the other 49 to say, 'I could have played that part.'**" Or "**How many Hollywood interior decorators does it take to trim a Christmas tree? Five: one to string the popcorn, one to flock the tree, one to put the Woolworth star on top, and two to stand back and say gaily, 'Oh girls, it's ssssoooo tacky.'**"

"Tacky material" (before it was called "politically incorrect" starting in the 1980s) was also popular early in his stand-up career: "**What are the first words a Mexican baby hears? 'Attention K-Mart Shoppers.'**" Or "**How did 500 Mexicans get to the Alamo? In two cars!**" If there were groans, and there often were, he would say "**Groans? Good. I was going for groans, and I got them! Great!**"

Then he would do more dated lines like "**Me with new material? Now THAT's funny. Like Divine** [or Shelley Winters or Mama Cass or any other then-current overweight celebrity] **dying of anorexia. Or like Brooke Shields with pencil-thin eyebrows. Or like Truman Capote wearing a T-shirt that said 'I choked Linda Lovelace.'**"

"**Me with new material? Ha! Come on. Are the landing lights still lit for Amelia Earhart? I don't THINK so.**"

"**I couldn't make up my mind when I came to Hollywood. Should I become a hairstylist or a high-class Beverly Hills hooker? So I flipped a coin. Heads or tails?** [Hold for laughs; the line always took awhile for the audience to get, then Charles would dead-pan:] **You know, I do ask you to <u>think</u> from time to time.**"

Two other longer "story" jokes, as opposed to his usual one-liners, often ended this first section of his show; in retrospect, both were quite telling. As Celene Kendall, Charles would confide:

"**People always want to know how I got my start in show business. Ok, I'll tell you. I was a teeny-tiny twat – oops, sorry, 'tot' – playing in mother's closet, swinging from hanger to hanger, when suddenly there was an earthquake. I was hurled into mother's high-heeled pumps, and a dress came cascading down off a hanger over my slender, child-like shoulders. What could I do, darling? I threw open the closet door, stepped out, and said 'Well, shit. I'm in show-biz!'**"

Or more accurately:

"**I did not go to my vocational guidance counselor in high school and say, 'Hi, I'd like to be a female impersonator.' She came to me and said, 'Charles, I've seen you in the hall. You're a female impersonator.' Well, at least I'm something.**"

He certainly was. "Something," that is.

But not really a "female impersonator."

Almost anyone can throw on women's clothing, a wig and makeup, or perform pantomimes to recordings. Charles Pierce developed a gifted comedian's rapier wit, a trained actor's vocal mimicry, visual parodies of celebrities' mannerisms, clever costumes and stylishly appropriate wigs, plus a cunning writer's kind of material – one-liners, stories, jokes, dialogue – that any of his famous ladies *might* have said in their appearances.

But he did his comedy material with intelligent humor, flamboyant theatricality, and campy enthusiasm.

He truly was a "**Male Actress.**"

Charles as his *nom-de-drag* Celene Kendall, Venetian Room, San Francisco, 1984

Charles as Mae West (above and at right), 1971

CHAPTER 3

MAE WEST

"**Oh, I feel like a million tonight. But I'll take 'em two at a time**," Charles-as-Mae would say, unless it was a particularly responsive audience. Then the line became "**But I'll take 'em ten at a time**." Or more.

Charles's ability to "work" a live audience became as legendary as the ladies he chose for his impressions. He perfected his timing and the order of his show over the years, so immediately after each glamorous opening that featured the Hollywood blondes, he would leave the stage, make a frantically fast 20-second (or less) costume change, all the while calmly continuing to speak as his own announcer via a strategically placed backstage microphone.

He would then saunter slowly back onstage, after announcing the special appearance, usually "**tonight only**," of "**Miss June West: Mae's sister, one month hotter**."

The quick change and outlandish costume got the first laugh. White leather and rhinestone holsters were sewn at each hip of a form-fitting, floor-length, red and silver sequined gown. The blonde wig under the big hat was a replica of Mae West's signature "up-do" with a top knot circled on his head.

As the Mae/June ensemble developed over the years, the cowboy hat went away, and sticking out of the wig was a single yellow turkey feather, looking like an unruly cowlick, which he referred to as "Tweetie bird." He often wore more pearls and beads than a Mardi Gras float, and dragged along a fluffy red-and-white turkey-feather boa, easily 25 feet long.

He would slither up to the microphone stand, flipping the boa, fake-primping the back of the wig with his hand as if to tame it, and calming the crowd's hysteria with Mae's sexually suggestive, guttural "Oh" (pronounced as a two-syllable *OH-ew*, which started almost every line his Mae said). He would roll his big eyes, plant his constantly gyrating hips in one place, and purr into the microphone one of his many almost-as-if-stolen-from-Mae risqué openers like "**Oh. Is that a gun you're totin', or are you just happy to see me?**," already getting flirtatious with a hot guy in the audience that one of his glamorous blondes had spotted earlier in the show. "**Oh, hello handsome. Why dontcha see me up and come sometime?** [Wait for it.] **I'm E.T.'s sister: E.Z.**"

"**Hello boys. Hello girls. Hello boy-girls. Hello girl-boys. I guess that covers everyone in the place. After all, this is San Francisco** [or Hollywood, or New York, or anywhere he performed that was gay-friendly]. **Oh honey, if fairies could fly, San Francisco would be a mile high.**"

"**I just got back from San Diego where I met a 21-inch admiral. Oh, wouldn't ya know, that turned out to be a television set. Then I stopped by Disneyland and while I was walking around trying to decide what to do with my 'A' coupons** [both lines dated the act], **I came to a wall that said 'Walt Disney Presents Dirty Storybook Land,' so I went right in. There was Snow White, bawling** [pause for innuendo] **her eyes out. She said 'Miss West, I can't stand it; I just stepped on a buttercup and now the dwarves won't let me eat butter for a month.' Oh Snow, I said, you'd better not tell the dwarves I just stepped on a cockroach.**"

"**Oh look at all this... I couldn't decide what to wear tonight, so I wore everything.**"

"**See this necklace?** [huge and gaudy] **It's where rhinestones go to die. And don't.**"

"**Oh, with all this horse-hair** [referring to the wig or shoulder pads], **whalebone** [corset], **and foam rubber** [full, "falsie" breasts forcing his own chest into the appearance of cleavage], **I don't know whether I'm a great star or a five-piece room group at Levitz Warehouse. Oh, I might actually be a sectional.**" Charles could make even the word "sectional" sound sensual and sexual, or a combination of the two.

He would often flip the rest of the long boa out from off stage, and in a voice half-way between Mae and Charles, would refer to the clever costume accessory by seeming to ad-lib "**Oh, if I had anything that long, I wouldn't have to be a female impersonator.**" Again, not the moniker he would have preferred as Charles Pierce, but the sexually charged line delivered as Mae got a long, knowing laugh.

His Mae/June character was the raunchiest that the man ever got onstage. He could spew out some of his bluest material, lurking behind the steamy image of Hollywood's original blonde bombshell sexpot. It was Charles-as-Mae/June that could cruise a hunk in the front row, often one sporting a rise in his Levi's, and make an aside to another hot guy sitting nearby with "**Oh look, his pants are so tight, I can practically see his religion. He's a Christian Scientist; he** *thinks* **it's big. Is that all you, honey, or did your hernia belt slip?**"

"**Oh, I was sitting at the bar the other night, wearing my skin-tight Dale Evans orthopedic Levi's, when a good-lookin' guy came up and said, 'Hey Miss West, how do you get into those?' Oh, I said, you could start by buying me a drink.**"

As the wife of famed TV cowboy Roy Rogers, Ms. Evans was known as a prissy prude, whom neither Charles nor Mae liked much. "**I call Dale Evans 'Miss Happy Trails.' You can see them on her face. Put your**

Charles as Mae West doing "station breaks" on KQED-TV in San Francisco, c. 1980

dentures in backwards, Dale, and bite your head off. She did. Looked better. But not much."

Dale became the butt of another one of Charles' jokes: "**Oh, I was sitting at the bar last night, enjoying my cocktail and a cigarette, and next to me was Dale Evans, who said 'Miss West, that's disgusting. I'd rather commit adultery than smoke in public.' Oh, I shot right back and said: So would I, honey. So would I.**"

Charles was big on innuendo ("*In-a-uendo*: **that's Italian for Preparation H**," he ad-libbed once ["**Write that down!**"], then added it to the show permanently). The more double entendres he could throw into a Mae West line, the happier he and his audiences were.

"**I was in Las Vegas at a poker table, and the tall, dark, and handsome croupier said 'Hey, Miss West, I'd like to lay you ten-to-one.' Oh, that's an odd time, I said, but I'll be there.**"

"**I went to the doctor for my annual physical, and he said 'Miss West, you have acute angina.' Oh, I said, thanks Doc, I always thought it was kinda cute myself.**"

"**He asked if I smoked after sex. I don't know; I never looked.**"

"**He told me to have patience. Oh Doc, I said. I've had every patient on the floor.**"

"**W.C. Fields once commented on my ample bosoms popping out of my tight dress. 'Goodness, Mae,' he said. 'Cover those up!' Oh shut up W.C. and calm down, I said; goodness has nothing to do with it. Why dontcha cool off with a glass of ice water? 'No thanks, Mae,' replied W.C. 'I never drink water. Fish fuck in it.'**

"**W.C. asked me once if I preferred Browning or Kipling. Oh, I don't know, W.C., I retorted. I've never kipled.**" (Again: "**You've got to know what I'm talking about...**")

"**Sex is a misdemeanor. D'more you miss, d'meaner you get**. (His witty mother Jessie also gave him that line.)

"**Sex is like air. It suddenly becomes very important when you're not getting any**.

"**Sex is like Bridge. If you don't have a good partner, you better have a good hand. Oh, and isn't it the ultimate rejection when that hand falls asleep?**

"I haven't had sex in so long... [The audience would usually reply: "How long?"] Well, if my gynecologist planted a lump of coal in there, it would be a diamond in the morning. Oh. Men are like diamonds, you know. They're never too big or too hard."

"If I could find a man as butch as Sigourney Weaver, I'd marry him. She rolls her own tampons, you know. She can even jump-start her own dildo. Oh... a dildo: that's a pickled deer.

"We'll take a short break here while you figure that one out."

"I don't have a lover. Just going to bed with myself is hard enough.

"I went to a Gay '90s party the other night. All the men were gay and all the women were 90.

"I'm on heavy drugs right now. I ate a pharmacist earlier today. Oh, I tried smoking pot, but the handle caught in my throat.

"Oh, I was 14 before I discovered that French was also a language."

"I was in a coffee shop last week, and the waitress asked me how I liked my coffee. Oh honey, I replied, I like my coffee like I like my men [the same set-up for the usual "strong and black" retort]. 'Well, I'm sorry, Miss West,' she interrupted, 'but we don't serve gay coffee.'

"Oh, I've had so many facelifts, I'm not speaking with my original mouth. I bend over and yawn."

"Do you like the dress, boys? It kept me out of the war. I won't say which one, but the South lost.

"Ah yes, the Civil War. I was with Grant when he took Richmond. And Richmond loved it."

"How do I keep my youth? In a cage, honey, a cage.

"Oh, you know: it's not about the men in my life. It's about the life in my men.

"The worst thing about being an atheist is that you have nothing to say during an orgasm.

"How do you find an old man in the dark? Oh, it's not hard.

"Why don't Mormons have sex standing up? Because it might lead to dancing."

"What's the difference between sensual and kinky? Sensual is with just the tip of the feather. Kinky is with the whole chicken."

"What's the difference between oh and ah? Four inches."

As with all the characters he did in his act, Charles would rarely use actual lines from their movies, but he had one classic Mae West favorite, from the infamous *Myra Breckenridge*, that he just couldn't resist. Mae meets a towering cowboy, and asks him how tall he is. "Six foot, seven inches, ma'am," he replies. "Oh," Mae coos, "never mind about the six feet. Let's talk about the seven inches."

"I was sitting at the bar the other night with my pet parakeet perched on my head [referring to the Tweetie-bird feather sticking out the top of the wig's bun], and announced to the guys around me that I'd go to bed with the first one who could guess the weight of my parakeet. 'Two thousand pounds,' one dumb hunk blurted out. Oh, that's close enough, I said. Let's go."

"What's my definition of the perfect lover? A man who can make mad, passionate love to you till four o'clock in the morning, then turn into a pizza."

"Oh, see this face, honey? It's leaving town in 20 minutes. Be on it."

"I played a lady sheriff once in a picture, with 400 gorgeous men in my posse. [pause for innuendo] I said 'posse.' We met Sitting Bull, and his wife Lying Cow. Sitting Bull came right at me with his deadly Indian weapon drawn to the hilt. Naturally I looked down, and saw there was a knot tied on the end of it. Oh Sitting Bull, I said. How come?"

"What's easier: being black or gay? Black. You don't have to tell your mother. Oh, and do you remember when 'black power' meant prune juice?"

Again, Charles rarely told story jokes in his show, usually opting for faster-paced one-liners. But a few longer stories often made it into the act, sometimes as "closers" of the Mae/June segment...

"Oh, I don't even know what I'm doing up here on stage. I'm dead! I went to heaven and checked in with St. Peter, who told me that I had to be very careful here: 'If you have dirty thoughts your wings will crumple and fall off.' So I decided to check that out. I walked seductively past a sailor and a marine. The sailor took one look at me, and his wings crumpled and fell off. As he bent over to pick them up, the marine's wings crumpled and fell off."

"I was looking out my bedroom window today, and my chauffeur Pedro was working on the Rolls Royce. I called down to him, 'Pedro,' I said. 'Stop polishing the car and come up to my bedroom.' Pedro came up to my bedroom. I said 'Pedro, take off my dress.' So Pedro pulled off my dress. Oh, I said, 'Now Pedro, take off my garters and my hose.' He slipped off my garters and my hose. 'Oh, now my panties and my bra.' Pedro removed my panties and my bra. I said, 'Ok, now Pedro, the next time I catch you wearing my clothes, you're fired.'"

Charles as Mae West sporting her "Tweetie bird top-knot." c.1980

"Oh, I was traveling out west, where men are men, and the sheep know it. I was in a stagecoach with Liberace, who was on his way to Hollywood to shoot a movie called *I Married a Woman*, a science-fiction horror film. We went through an Indian reservation and met a gay Indian: a sweet Sioux. Oh, 'Yippee-ky-oh, K-Y.'

"Jesse James held up the coach, and said 'Ok, girls, pass everything you've got out the window.' Oh, I said, JJ, what I've got's too big to go out any window. Then Jesse pleased me – and Liberace – saying that what he had was too big to go *in* any window. He announced he was going to rob all the women and rape all the men. Oh, you're out of your mind, JJ, I said. Don't you have that in reverse? That's when Liberace piped up from the rear of the coach and said gaily, 'Oh shut up, Mae. Let Jesse rob the coach the way she wants to!'"

"I was moseying through a cow pasture when a bull started chasing me. I was tired, so I ran. [Hold for laughs.] I made it to the fence and jumped over. [Hold again.] There was an old farmer standing there who asked, 'Hey there, lady, what's the matter? Can't ya take it?' Oh, of course I can take it, I said, but what would I do with a calf in a three-room apartment?"

The eruption of laughter usually gave him enough time to sashay off stage, with the long boa trailing behind, slowly following him offstage. Sometimes we had a backstage helper take the boa from Charles after he got off stage and out of sight, and the helper would continue to pull the long boa gradually off stage as if Mae were still dragging it behind her, while the applause and laughter continued, and the next introduction would start.

All the while making the fast costume change, Charles kept talking from the backstage microphone, transitioning from Mae/June's voice into Charles/Celine's, then into the unmistakably wavering warble of Katharine Hepburn introducing herself.

By the time Mae's boa was finally disappearing off stage, Charles would step over it as he walked on as Kate Hepburn, adding to the quick-change-inspired illusion that there were more than one of him in the act.

Charles in another "generic Hollywood blonde" pose, which could have been anyone from Carol Channing to Mae West, depending on how many costume changes he felt like making during any particular show or engagement. Changing wigs was easier.

Charles as Katharine Hepburn in *The Lion in Winter*, 1985

CHAPTER 4

Katharine Hepburn

" was fascinated when I arrived at the theatre today and realized that Dorothy Pavilion's middle name was Chandler."

This unexpected and unplanned ad-lib started Charles's shaky-voiced Katharine Hepburn section of the glitzy extravaganza that he first headlined in April 1974 at the grand Los Angeles concert hall and opera house of its downtown Music Center, site for years of the Academy Awards ceremonies and telecasts. During the show, and for years after, Charles and most of his characters referred to the huge Dorothy Chandler Pavilion as "Dottie's Place." The show was such a success that it was reprised, and recorded on film, at the DCP in 1982.

[Search for "Charles Pierce Uncensored" on YouTube (https://youtu.be/KMV2DuwjGpM) to get glimpses of Charles's many characters, and their ability to play such a huge theatre.]

By the time Ms. Hepburn had started showing signs of Parkinson's (although she reportedly insisted that it was not actually Parkinson's), she became fodder for Charles's good-natured take on the great actress, which he included as the pre-intermission segment of his raucous charade-in-a-parade of Hollywood legends at the Chandler. In fact, during a majority of the nightclub shows he did from 1970 to 1990, his Kate Hepburn was the penultimate segment, usually following Mae West, and preceding the Bette Davis finale.

: : : : :

Charles as Joan Collins, 1984

During the popular "Dynasty" series on TV, Charles added a Joan Collins segment to the show, in place of Katharine Hepburn, for a few years in the mid- to late-'80s. But as he said, doing Joan with a thick-for-effect faux British accent, "**I don't *do* anything. I just wear clothes. I cahn't sing. I cahn't dance. And don't you dare say I cahn't act**.

"**My acting has been compared to Nell Carter pole vaulting. And they say all those naughty things about me, like what do I put behind my ears to attract men? My legs! That I've had more hands up my dress than The Muppets. That they call me the 'British Open.'**

"**I DO take care of myself. I eat healthy. No liqueurs. And I only smoke one cigarette after sex. I'm down to four packs a day. I'm not bisexual, but if you buy me something, I'll be sexual.**"

His Joan Collins impression was so good, the producers of a "Dean Martin Celebrity Roast" of Ms. Collins flew Charles to Las Vegas to appear at the NBC taping of the event in 1984. With Joan Collins herself seated on the dais, Charles-as-Joan said, "**I'm like a Tom Collins, but without the cherry.**" Joan howled; she loved him. In some of the photographs taken of the two backstage, it was difficult to tell them apart.

When Charles appeared on the bill with The Incomparable Hildegarde at Carnegie Hall in 1986, Cardinal John O'Connor stormed out of the show when Charles got a bit too raunchy as Joan Collins. Unfazed and unflustered, Charles dug an old line out of his mental trove of religious material and reminded the Cardinal that the last time Joan saw him at the cathedral's high mass, she had said to him that "**I love your drag, sweetie, but your purse is on fire.**" The Cardinal was not amused.

Even though *The New York Times*' review of Charles's 1988 opening at the Ballroom called Joan Collins his funniest segment, she didn't last long in the act. Neither did a short skit he did as Eva Peron during the *Evita* era. **"Don't cry for me, Altadena; the truth is I never liked you."**

The truth is that audiences preferred his Kate Hepburn, so she was soon back in the act full-time, replacing those "upstarts."

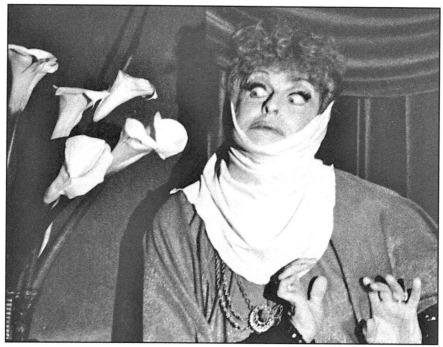

Charles as Katharine Hepburn in *The Lion in Winter,* at San Francisco's Plush Room, 1985

Dressed in a simple coolie jacket and black pants, Charles strode onto the Dorothy Chandler Pavilion stage as Kate, carrying a bouquet of white calla lilies. He and his team of brilliant costume designers had a white cowl with a shock of unruly henna wig peeking out in front, and only his face showing, surrounded by the shoulder-length nun's habit. He looked exactly like Hepburn in *The Lion in Winter*, and sounded like her too, shaky vocal delivery and all....

"Lion in winter. Pussy in summer. It was a busy year at the castle. I was Eleanor of Aqua-Net, uh, sorry: Aquitaine, married to King Henry of Surrey, with the fringe on top. Ha ha: a bit of humor I put in there. And I had three children: Richard the Lionhearted. Claude the Chicken-hearted. And Maid Marion, the Undecided.

"**Claude designed mother's costume. I think Claude was probably gay, but we didn't call it that then. We certainly didn't have gay bars in the eleven-hundreds. All the bars were glum. Imagine going to your first glum bar. No fun**.

"**King Henry was a bisexual; he liked sex twice a year. I gave him a medieval vasectomy, and every time he got excited, the drawbridge went up. Remember that scene in the picture? I said 'Every family has its up and downs.' We all talked like that in the twelfth century. I held up my jewels and said that I would hang them from the nipples but it would upset the children. So I did. But they weren't. What's a mother to do? Fuck the kids, I say**."

Charles rarely dropped the F-bomb, especially at so tony and hallowed a place as the Dorothy Chandler Pavilion. But he did it because he could, because he believed that part of what made comedy funny was the unexpected. It was surreally funny having Katharine Hepburn swear, especially as the medieval Eleanor of Aquitaine. It "worked" at the Chandler, but worked better in more intimate nightclubs.

"**Well so much for 'Lying in Winter'**," he announced, removing the cowl headdress, revealing a typically Hepburn frizzy bunhead wig. He would walk upstage to the piano and deposit the headdress, then, as he walked back toward the microphone stand, his myopic Kate would mistake the thin stand for a thin "**Cher? Is that you?**" He would then look up at the very top balcony of the huge theatre and say "**I must look like a garbanzo bean on a neck from up there in $2.50.**" That was sign of the times in 1974: admission to a Dorothy Chandler Pavilion concert was only $2.50, albeit in the top balcony.

(Another sign of the times, and inflation: during the opening segment of his reprised concert at the DCP eight years later in 1982, Charles welcomed the crowd with "**Well hello again. Your over-the-hill Valley Girl is here. That's Death Valley**. [Addressing the top balcony again:] **How's the makeup up there in $7.50?**")

But back to shaky Kate…

"**Now what about my other pictures?** *Guess Who's Coming To Throw Up Dinner? On Goldie Hawn…* **Sorry:** *On Golden Pond. Suddenly Last Summer. The African Queen.* (Aside to an unsuspecting fan: "**No one you'd know, dear**.") (Laughter from this line prompted this response:)

"Ok, what's so funny about an African Queen?"

"Remember *The Glass Menagerie*? I had that dumb daughter Laura. She didn't know the difference between escargots and boogers. I asked her once, 'Laura, how many feet in a yard?' She said, 'I don't know, Mother. How many people are *in* the yard?'"

"**Do you like my hair, dear?**" he would ask no one in particular, mock-fluffing Kate's unkempt curly bird's-nest wig. "**Sebastian from *Suddenly Last Summer* designed it, you know. It wasn't really even a 'hair-do.' More like a 'hair-don't.' Ah, my son Sebastian. So gay. 'How gay was Sebastian?,' someone may query. They might even 'ask.' Sebastian was so gay he'd had his entire body tattooed as a Gucci bag. Now that's pretty damn gay**.

"**In the picture, I had a house in New Orleans. Everybody did. Outside the house we had a little garden. Everybody did. In the garden was a little gazebo… a small hutch actually. It might have been a Doggie Diner for all I know. But every afternoon Sebastian and I would sit there and have a 5-o'clock Dyke-ery** [that's daiquiri, mispronounced]… **which was a small New Orleans lesbian. They're only about that tall. As they'd walk away from you, you'd say 'Isn't that Paul Williams?'**

"**I knew little Paul, you know. One day he came up to me and said, 'Miss Hepburn, I would love to make love to you.' Well, I looked down at him and said, 'If you do, Paul, and I ever *hear* about it…'**"

"**Spencer Tracy and I went camping once, and decided to have some fun, so we jumped over the campfire. He was blackballed and I was deferred.**" [It helped to actually hear that 'de-furred' pun.]

"**Yes, there were all those films, and then there was the Broadway musical I did, called *Coco*. Pearl Bailey did the matinées; then they called it *Hot Chocolate*. I played Coco: Gabrielle Chanel, the great dress designer in the '20s. She gave the world costume jewelry. Thank God, or I wouldn't have been here earlier** [referring to himself as Mae West]. **Coco Chanel put women into simple basic black dresses and she put them into slacks, which pleased the other women already wearing them.**

"**Gertrude Stein used to come to my Parisienne salon day after day, saying things like** [in a deep voice:], "**Right on, Coco. A slack is a slack is a slack.**"

[Back to Kate's warble:] "**I had to tell her to go. She scared the hell out of me.**"

After the laughter subsided, it suddenly got very quiet in the house as the lights dimmed, and Charles continued the serious but still playful story of Coco Chanel.

"**As a child, as Coco, I lived in a cold gray house, with two cold gray aunts. My father was a champagne salesman, and like his product, just as bubbling and disappearing. He came to me just before my communion day, and said – in a very high, very feminine voice – 'Oh Gabrielle. Yoo hoo, Gabby?' That was daddy's voice. He was suspect in the provinces. But so admired in the city.**

"**We mustn't make fun of daddy's voice you know. He suffered terribly from an accident as a child when a toilet seat fell on his throat. And someone was on it!**

"**Daddy asked me what color dress I wanted for my first communion, and I said 'Oh daddy, could it be red?** [pronounced as a shaky two-syllable *ray-edd*] **Could it be, daddy? Huh, huh? And green, and purple, and polka-dotted?' Daddy liked the idea; he had one made up for himself, and left. We never saw daddy again.**

"**I grew up. I went to Paris where I became rich and famous. But always a 'mademoiselle.'** *No one after whom I'm always cleaning...*"

[Music started. Lights lowered to just his face.]

"*Without whom, life would barely have a meaning. No one. There was no one…*"

After almost an hour of a show with high hilarity and raucous laughter, suddenly Charles got dramatic. He loved singing this song, because his not-always-pitch-perfect voice matched Kate Hepburn's similar delivery, and the lyrics applied appropriately to all three of them: Coco Chanel, Katharine Hepburn, and Charles Pierce.

Seemingly channeling Hepburn channeling Chanel, Charles sang and acted the brilliant "Always Mademoiselle" from Alan Jay Lerner and Andre Previn's 1969 musical *Coco*, which Ms. Hepburn had performed on that same stage of the Dorothy Chandler Pavilion a few years before Charles's first concert there.

Clever mademoiselle. Brilliant mademoiselle.
Everything that mattered she scattered away.
Dazzling mademoiselle. In her golden shell.
Life is such a merry, but solitary holiday.
Gone. Gone is all the love, she had so much of.
Never more to be, never more will she cast another spell.

Who the devil cares just what a woman wears?
Is it worth a stitch, ending up a witch, in a golden hell?
One is as one does, and by God it was,
Life was as it had to be.
It was not too bad to be, always mademoiselle.
Right or wrong, I'm glad to be...
Gabrielle Chanel!

Between Charles's dramatic build at the end of the song and the movie-score-with-violins-rich orchestra behind him, the song's end and blackout brought the 3,000+ members of the sold-out Dorothy Chandler Pavilion audience to its collective feet with a spontaneous, opera-length ovation, even longer than the one that had followed the show's overture, his introduction, and first entrance in full glamour drag.

That original 1974 DCP concert was not only the highlight of his career, it was also its midpoint. The *Los Angeles Times* review of the show raved about him as "America's quintessential female impersonator" ["No, no, no: '**Male Actress**!'" you could almost hear Charles whimper], noting that "in the 16 years he had played nightclubs and cabarets mainly patronized by the gay contingent," now here he was, in the early gay-lib days, performing on the Music Center stage.

Ironically, probably due to royalty restrictions, the 1982 filmed "encore" of his 1974 Music Center show did not include the show-stopping "Always Mademoiselle" number, even though the voice-over on the YouTube version of it announces the evening as the "Uncensored" (but not uncut) version of "The Legendary Ladies of the Silver Screen."

Also ironically, Charles's career lasted exactly another 16 years.

It was now intermission.

Charles as Bette Davis as Margo Channing in *All About Eve*, c. 1985

CHAPTER 5

BETTE DAVIS

"**I**'d like to do a scene for you from all of my films.**"

As with all Charles's impressions/parodies of popular movie stars of the day, his Bette Davis was physically spot-on and wickedly clever. It was also his most astute, accurate, and hysterically funny. He LOOKED like Bette – same bugged eyes, pursed lips, neurotic, erratic walk and arm twirl (if slightly exaggerated), with the ever-present cigarette – and when he came on stage in an exact replica of Miss Davis's iconic off-the-shoulder black satin dress and wig from *All About Eve* (at left), jaws would drop at his likeness to the great star.

At the Encore Theatre during *Geese*'s "Cabaret Mondays" in 1970, we had talked about what fun it would be – while Charles was changing out of his Katharine Hepburn outfit into Bette Davis – to show that famed *All About Eve* clip where Bette-as-Margo Channing came down her stairs for the party, stopped at the landing, and delivered her famous line, "Fasten your seat belts, it's going to be a bumpy night."

At legendary Ciro's nightclub on the famed Sunset Strip in Los Angeles during our first engagement there later that year, we got that chance. We constructed a movie screen on stage, made with six-inch wide vertical strips of elastic bandages. An old friend of mine in charge of some film archives lent us a 16mm copy of *All About Eve*, and we projected that brief film clip. Just after Ms. Davis did her 'bumpy night' line, the film paused on her image, and through the Ace-bandage screen stepped Charles, dressed, wigged, and made-up exactly like Bette-as-Margo. The visual was boggling, and the entrance got a screaming ovation every night.

The cheering usually went on for at least a minute or so, during which Charles would swagger around the stage, twirl his arms, purse his lips, puff a cigarette, bug his eyes, stop and glare, and have a sip of a drink, all the while filling the time until the crowd calmed down. Then he would dead-pan: "**Thaaan-kew. So you *do* know who I am?**" More hysteria.

Another lasting memory of "the Bette entrance" occurred in 1981 when the Merola Opera program, educational wing of San Francisco Opera, asked me to produce a fundraising event at Club Fugazi, where *Beach Blanket Babylon* had been performing since 1975 (and as of 2016, was still going strong, 40+ years later). Angela Lansbury was in San Francisco at the time, appearing in *Sweeney Todd*, and she had agreed to headline our benefit. But just a week before the Merola event, Angela called to say that her show would be closing unexpectedly early; she had to leave town before our event, and could not be part of the Fugazi fund-raiser after all.

Desperate to replace Angela in less than a week, I decided to ask Charles if he might appear in her stead. Always up for a challenge, he agreed. We decided to try a special "surprise" approach to revealing that night that Ms. Lansbury would not be there. Before the audience could express any disappointment, the evening's glamorous soprano emcee excitedly announced that "Instead, we are fortunate to have with us tonight another great lady of the silver screen. Ladies and gentlemen, you all know this great legend… please welcome Miss Bette Davis!"

The place came unglued, and the 300 society members in attendance gasped *en masse* when *All About Eve* Bette came on stage, greeted the ovation with those big bugged eyes, twirling arms, and Davis swagger, wearing that famous cocktail dress, this time in bright red. When the emcee, wearing an elegant gown of the exact same red, left the stage, Charles-as-Bette over-reacted to her similarly colored gown, and stomped off stage in mock horror.

Over the raucous applause and general hysteria, the off-stage emcee announced, "Ladies and gentlemen, Mister Charles Pierce," who returned to a deafening ovation (by then he was a local legend). He did 20 minutes of the best Bette material he had, replete with opera references provided by his dresser/costume designer Herman George (also a costumer and dresser at the San Francisco Opera and *BBB*). It all resulted in spontaneous laughs and cheers, especially satisfying considering the audience was comprised of wealthy, urbane, stereotypically stuffy opera supporters. And they were all convinced, at least for about a minute after "she" was announced, that Bette Davis herself was actually there. The surprise and resulting levity assuaged any disappointment about Angela Lansbury not being there.

Charles-as-Bette was always the highlight of his show. She was bitchy and exaggerated, and usually had not-very-nice things to say about other actresses like Joan Crawford (remember "**She's dead** [tet]. **Goot.**"?). By changing just facial and vocal expression, (s)he would launch into recreating a few scenes, with Charles's "take" on some of the lines from *What Ever Happened to Baby Jane?*, switching back and forth between Bette as "Baby" Jane Hudson and Joan Crawford as her sister Blanche. "**Oh Jane, there's an old dead bird on my tea tray.**"

"**Yeah, it's *tet*, Blanche. And I basted it in Pepsi.**" (You may recall that Joan Crawford's husband was president of PepsiCo at the time, and she did publicity for the company.)

"**Eat it, Blanche! Or wouldja maybe like a tongue sandwich?**

"**Oh Jane, you know I never eat anything out of an animal's mouth.**

"**Really, Blanche? Then wouldja like some eggs?** [Wait for it.]

"**Oh Jane, try to be nice. You wouldn't treat me this way if I wasn't a cripple in a wheelchair.**

"**But cha are, Blanche. Ya ARE.**" More often than not, especially after devoted fans had made repeated returns to a CP performance, the audience would recite the "**But cha are, Blanche**" line along with him.

As Joan: "**Oh Jane, Why don't you compliment me once in awhile?**" As Bette: "**Aw bullshit Blanche. That would be like sewing a sequin on a rat's ass. If you're looking for sympathy you'll find it in the dictionary between 'shit' and 'suicide'.**" Technically it wasn't, but when I pointed that out, Charles wouldn't change it. The line was so unexpectedly funny, no one else ever noticed the literary inaccuracy, or said anything if they did. And he got another laugh with "**And I wish you'd do one or the other!**"

When dial phones were still being used, and if an audience was with him, Charles would pantomime Bette-as-Jane dialing the phone to call in an order from Johnson's Liquors. After a long time dialing, Charles would dead-pan into the phone: "**Outside line please,**" then proceed to order "**Six bottles of bourbon, a vat of vodka, and a Hostess Ding Dong. Oh, and a six-pack of Pepsi for Blanche.**"

Joan Crawford would often butt in and take over, demanding equal time with Bette. Joan would scream (and encourage fans to scream along with) the line from *Mommie Dearest*: "**No. More. Wire. Hangers! Ever!**" Charles-as-Joan might also spew lines such as "**Christina, your Mommie Dearest has your bath water ready. I've had it boiling for two weeks.**"

Joan Crawford had recently died, and because Charles wanted to expand his normal show for the Chandler encore engagement in 1982, Joan

got her own pre-Bette section of the show, dressed in a '40s boudoir gown with shoulder pads. It was brief and bitchy, especially about Joan's daughter Christina (from *Mommie Dearest*), but apparently Bette got impatient backstage, and took over from Joan rather quickly.

Charles ended the Bette segment with one of the "tightest" Bette/Joan back-and-forth banters, incorporating some of the above lines, and adding Bette saying "**Joan's *tet* you know. But she will not lie down, and she'll never let**

Charles as Joan Crawford in *Mommie Dearest*

us forget she's *tet*. In 'Baby Jane' she was sick. She was old. She was tired. She was sick and tired of being old. She was a cripple in a wheelchair. Pity. She always got upset when I did jokes about her. 'What's the hardest thing to eat in a vegetable?' I'd ask. 'The wheelchair'!" Clearly, political correctness had not yet caught on in 1982.

Charles researched and re-read some of his old Gilded Cage comedy material to find lines he had forgotten, and came up with a routine for the DCP encore that he had used in the early '70s when he was expanding his act. It was an exchange inspired by the 1962 *Baby Jane* film, with Charles-as-Bette-as-Baby Jane reminding Joan/Blanche of the time…

"**I was nice to you once, Blanche. I took you to San Francisco in your wheelchair. Remember? I pushed you all the way up Highway 5, before it was open** [in 1971]. **I took you to the top of Lombard Street, that crookedy little tourist street, and gave your wheelchair a push. What fun you had, diggin' your spiked wedgies into the concrete, sending sparks up over Coit Tower. You landed in the nets at Fisherman's Wharf and even gave the crabs crabs.**

"Remember what happened next, Miss Showbiz? [As Joan:] Why yes. Yes I do, Jane. [Back to Bette:] A seagull flew right overhead and did do-do all over your face. [As Joan, pantomiming wiping bird-do off her face:] I said run, Jane, quickly, and get the toilet paper. [As Bette:] WHAT are you talking about, Blanche?"

Right then Bette turned into Tallulah Bankhead doing a variation on her famed "Acting with Tallulah" record album, where she reads the same line with several different emphases. So Charles-as-Bette-as-Tallulah overacts, saying, "What ARE you talking about? What are you TALKING about? What are you talking ABOUT?"

[Then back as Bette/Jane-to-Joan/Blanche about the seagull poop:] "Really, Blanche: by the time I got back with the toilet paper, that bird's ass would be halfway across the Pacific." [Wait for it.]

That exchange ended the Bette segment of the DCP encore concert in 1982, after which Charles came back for his final bow and announced that this show was actually his First Annual Final Farewell Engagement. As it turned out, he did eight more years of them.

Back to Bette again in his regular nightclub show: "I'll never forget my pictures, and I'll never let YOU forget my pictures! NOW I'd like to do a scene for you from all of my films.

"My favorite line from all my pictures was from *Cabin in the Cotton* when I said 'I'd love to kiss ya, but I just washed my hair.'" [pronounced, of course, *hay-yah*]

"And what about those stinkers I made? In *Beyond the Forest* I played Rosa Moline, a 12 o'clock gal in a 9 o'clock town, waiting for 2 a.m., with 5 o'clock shadow. There I was, leaving my small town – Kansas City, New Mexico – craawwwling up the railroad tracks to Chicago with Peritonitis: some Greek I'd picked up in a bar. The town was so small, there was just a one-way street through it. If you missed your exit, you had to drive around the world to get back home. The tide went out one day, and never came back. The Avon Lady was so dumb, instead of ringing your doorbell, she'd 'tinkle' on your front lawn.

"There was only one gay bar: Chez Dorothy's. They had a Sunday brunch followed by a short little drag pantomime show. The one female impersonator was a woman!... Debbie Reynolds!"

To continue doing "a scene for you from all of my films," Bette would "**remember a picture I made** [*mate*] **called** [*calt*] ***Dead Ringer*** [*Tet Rheenghuh*]. **I played twins named Margaret and Edie** [*EEE-tee*]. **Margaret was rich. Edie was poor. Tough. She ran a dyke bar on Figueroa. Edie killed** [*kilt*] **Margaret because she had a LOT more money… an excellent reason for killing anyone. And I took Margaret's place. But I was found out by Jim the detective, so I said to him, 'Jim the detective: look, I'm not Margaret, I'm EEE-tee. Dontcha know me, Jim? Dontcha?' He didn't.**

"**And what about** *Hush… Hush Sweet Charlotte*? **My GAWD, I was old in that one. Remember when I was sitting at the table, and barked:** [with a pause after each word] **What. Do. You. Think. I. Asked. You. Here. For? CUMP-nee? My cousin Miriam's coming to help me. SHE'll tell you to fuck off. She's in Public Relations, which sounds pretty dirty to me. She's a bull dyke, you know. She won't take 'yes' for an answer!**"

Another of Charles's favorite Bette Davis films was *The Star*, which he had seen so often as a student at Pasadena Playhouse that he started doing his impression of it for friends. "**I played Margaret Elliot, a famous movie star. On the skids. In the scene, I'm driving drunk through Beverly Hills, looking for Barbara Lawrence's home. Now I know what you're thinking: 'Who the fuck is Barbara Lawrence?' Well, I'll TELL you. She was a starlet who could kick her legs higher and wider than anyone in town. She could work Sunset and Vine, all four corners at the same time. How nice for Barbara.**

"**The cops stopped me and gave me a Breathalyzer test that sent the balloon up around the world. So I went to jail. But the next morning, like in all good Hollywood pictures, I was out. And working in the lingerie department of the May Company.**

"**I was waiting on two little old biddies from Pasadena, and, of course, one recognized me as the Oscar-winning actress. She says to her friend** (in a voice sounding a bit like Eleanor Roosevelt), '**Madge, look. That's Margaret Elliot. Why, she looks older than dirt. It's a disgrace for a store like this to employ a jailbird like her. I wouldn't buy a girdle in her department.'**

"**And I** *heard* **them** [with blinking, bug-eyed looks after each word]**. So I said, 'Cows don't** *wear* **girdles, and yes, it IS a disgrace, ladies: Margaret Elliot waiting on a couple of old bags like you.'**

"'WELL,' says the one old bag, 'you can't talk to us like that. I'll call the manager.'

"'CALL the manager! Call the president! Call me madam! I won't be here. I'm going back to where I can be Margaret Elliot.' Then I really let them have it. 'Back to my old job in the circus, shoveling up after elephants like you.'

"'Why, I've never been so insulted,' says one.

"Well, then you should get out more often!'"

:::::

At this point in the show, the drink that was pre-set on the piano had usually been sipped away, so Charles would exaggerate taking the last swallow, then toss the glass into the fireplace at Freddy's in New York, or against another nightclub's stage wall, shattering glass everywhere (safely, of course). After the audience finished gasping and laughing, he would calmly ask "**Don't you wish you could do that at *your* work?**"

He asked for another cocktail and when it arrived, Charles-as-Bette would sip it, do a spit-take, and dead-pan: "**That's AWful. It tastes like something you'd sit in to remove a tattoo! People say I have a drinking problem. Ha! I have no problem drinking at all!**"

Other impressionists would usually use one of Bette's alleged movie lines: "Peter, Peter, Peter." Charles did the research, watched all of the legend's films, and never once found a reference to anyone named Peter; but this didn't stop him from including it in his own variation: "**Petah, Petah, Petah... You really MUST change your name. How CAN I say across the breakfast table: 'Pass the salt Petah.'?**" Or as he ad-libbed once: "**Petah, Petah, Petah... I've really got to get myself some Petah.**"

His dialogue was at its sharpest when the back-and-forth involved Bette and her real-life arch-nemesis, Tallulah Bankhead. Charles had a great talent for switching voices and characters instantly. As Bette, he would look at the imaginary Tallulah by his side, bray a bitchy line, then during the laugh, turn his head, adjust the wig slightly to Tallulah's style, change his voice to her deeper drawl, and bark back at Bette. Charles-as-Bette explained that "**Tallulah always hated me because I played on film all the parts she made famous on Broadway. Well, except for the *Lifeboat* movie, when she played an oar.**" [Wait for it.]

And that started Charles's famous Bette/Tallulah bitch fight:

"I tried to be nice to Tallulah. I sent her a telegram once on her Broadway opening night. It said 'Kisses on your opening.'

"Bette! If you ever become a mother, may I have one of the puppies?

"Tallulah! You ARE one of the puppies. AND, you're actually *like* doggie-do: the older you get the easier you are to pick up.

"Oh Bette, you're such a smart ass. I'll bet you could sit on an ice cream cone and tell me the flavor.

"Tallulah! You should be nice to me. I had an affair with a buffalo once. You could be my daughter.

"Bette, is that a girdle you're wearing, or a retaining wall? And isn't that dandruff on your shoes?

"I love your dress, Tallulah. I always have. Now come on. Look at me. I have the body of a 16-year-old girl.

"Well then, Bette, you ought to give it back. You're wrinkling the shit out of it.

"Tallulah, you have a perfect voice for hog-calling.

"That's right, Bette. And here you are.

"Tallulah, Tallulah, Tallulah. Your mother called you 'Tallulah' because she couldn't spell [the sound of retching, something like:] 'bleauggghh.' Is it true that when you were born, the doctor slapped your mother?

"Oh really, Bette. Acid wouldn't melt your face.

"Tallulah! Is that your face or did your neck throw up?

"Oh Bette, dahling, if that's your skin, you've outlived it! May I suggest you try either moisturizer or wood filler?

"It's obviously time to have your hair done, Tallulah, but you're so old, there's no one alive who remembers the 'set'.

"Oh Bette, shut up and have a drink. You know that *I* only drink to pass away the time until I get drunk. Mine was the only blood test that came back with an olive in it. My husband never knew I was an alcoholic until I came home sober one night."

Depending on how lively and responsive the audience was, and what kind of mood Charles was in (most often feisty and energetically eager to please), the Bette/Joan or Bette/Tallulah exchange would go on, with new ad-libs and topical one-liners enhancing the dialogue.

On the night in 1980 when Angela Lansbury saw him at the Plush Room in San Francisco, Charles-as-Tallulah dragged a ratty old mink coat on stage, and did about ten of the funniest ad-libbed minutes ever, sitting/slumping on the piano, sipping a cocktail after each funny line. Somewhere out of the depths of his fertile mind came

Charles as Tallulah Bankhead

a new line (or possibly old, but new to me at the time): as Tallulah spread her legs, she barked at the closest audience member: "**Have you ever been this close to an open grave before?**" Angela nearly choked.

Charles appeared on Wayland Flowers' "Madame's Place" TV show in 1982, playing Madame's cousin Charley, a Vietnam veteran and country gentleman who had been living near a radiation plant. One night while he watched a Bette Davis movie, there was an accident at the plant; from then on, every time Charley heard the word "trash," he would turn into Bette Davis. This was clearly a thin plot gimmick, but what the hell, it was the then-popular "Madame's Place," and it got Charles on TV as a guest star to do some of his nightclub comedy material. Any publicity was good.

Charles-as-Charley appeared as a very glamorous Bette in several scenes, the first of which allowed him to look around Madame's "place," and do Bette's signature "What a dump!" line. Charles-as-Charley-as Bette and Madame also got to do a lot of the Bette-Tallulah bitch-fight dialogue, which worked for both of them. Charles even added one of the lines he sometimes used in his Bette-Tallulah back-and-forth in his club act: "**Madame! I passed your house the other day, and you must have been sunbathing. Vultures were circling overhead.**"

In Charles's act, Bette and Tallulah usually had a brief final moment. One was about the time Bette threw a cocktail party ("**We were all just sitting around, telling cock tales.**"). She ran out of caviar, so her maid had to serve the only thing she could muster: buckshot on Wheat Thins. Tallulah ate one too many, and had to go to the bathroom. When she came back to the party, she apologized to Bette for bumping into and knocking over one of her Ming vases as she came out of the toilet. "**Oh that's alright Tallulah. I have more.**"

"**No, no, Bette, dahling. Never mind the silly vase. When I bent over to pick up the pieces, I shot your cat!**"

Another crowd-pleasing story Charles often used was an unusually uncharacteristic story he would tell after a well-received Bette/Tallulah barrage. Charles-as-Bette sounded sentimental about a time they made up and were finally getting along. Bette was driving them from Hollywood for a desert weekend together in Palm Springs, when Tallulah said:

"**Bette dahling, you really must stop the car. I have to pee.** [as Bette:] **So I pulled over. Tallulah got out and went behind a large cactus. She really let go. It was a flood. A small lake formed. Swans floated by. Dolphins played. Esther Williams came out of retirement. The locals started building an ark. But just as Tallulah finished peeing mid-squat, a rattlesnake came along and bit her, right there in her Bermuda Triangle. 'Ouch,' she mumbled, then she brayed at me:**

"**Bette, burn rubber! Hurry and go get a doctor. Please save me!**"

"**So I sped off, then cruised leisurely into town, had lunch and a few cocktails, saw a movie,** *Gandhi*, **twice, got a manicure, pedicure, and massage, and finally found a doctor. He told me I'd have to take a knife, cut the wound, and suck out the poison. I turned into Barbara Stanwyck right there: 'Oh no, I cahn't; my lips are caught to my teeth. Oh no.' I didn't know what to do.**

"**So I slid behind the wheel, got gas, had the car lubed, washed, waxed, and polished, the tires rotated, and finally made it back to Tallulah, still hunched on the side of the road. She was desperate.**

"**Bette dahling, quick, tell me: what did the doctor say? I took a long drag on my cigarette, exhaled slowly, and announced emphatically: 'Tallulah. The doctor says** [pause, puff, exhale]… **you're going to die.'**"

One of Charles's earliest routines was based on his original nightclub act idea about what it would have been like if Bette Davis had played Scarlett O'Hara. He wrote his imaginary scene from *Gone with the Wind*, between Scarlett and Prissy, where Bette-as-Scarlett tells Prissy to run and get the tools for childbirth. Charles-as-Bette-doing-Prissy says, "**But Miss Scarlett, Miss Scarlett, I don't know nothin' about birthin' no babies. I's a lesbian. And Miss Scarlett, Miss Scarlett, the yankees are coming, the yankees are coming. They're going to burn Altanta!**

"**Oh, no! Really Prissy?**" an alarmed Charles-as-Bette-as-Scarlett responds. "**Then start packing. Pack everything. Pack the curtain-rod dress. Pack Melanie. Pack, pack, pack.**"

"**But Miss Scarlett, Miss Scarlett, I's scared. The yankees are coming and they're going to rape all the women!**"

"**Really Prissy?** [pause, puff, exhale] **Unpack.**"

Smoking in nightclubs was still permitted in the 1970s and 1980s, which was a good thing for his Bette. Ms. Davis herself always had a cigarette in hand, certainly on TV talk shows and other public appearances, and often on film, so Charles would make his first entrance as Bette with a lit cigarette, which lasted maybe five minutes into the act. He would then ask politely if anyone in the audience could spare another one. ("**I left mine in the machine.**") Some eager guy would always jump up and offer one. Charles would take it, look at it, and throw it back, barking a withering "**LIT!**" When the guy held up a match or lighter, Charles would bend over it and feign being burned, screaming "**Murderer! This wig is cheap. I could go up** (in flames) **like THAT!**"

And if the guy was attractive, Charles would add, flirtatiously: "**And I could go *down* like that too.**" Once again, "**You have to know what I'm talking about…**"

"**Thaaan-kew for the cigarette. And the light. How kind. But then I've always had to rely on the kindness of strangers. And you are a kind stranger. And this** [the cigarette] **could be a Rely** [a tampon]."

"**They say that for every cigarette you smoke, you lose two minutes off your life. I must call my doctor and tell him I died forty years ago!**"

Charles-as-Bette once appeared in a Gay Men's Chorus benefit at the grand new Davies Symphony Hall in San Francisco, and as usual, walked on with cigarette in hand. But even before he could start his "**Thaaan-kew**" routine, the house lights came on, as did the fire marshal, who stopped the show by walking up to Charles and saying, "Sorry, ma'am (!), but there's no smoking in the hall." "**Well! How rude!**" blasted Bette, firing off another instant ad-lib: "**Don't you know who I used to be?**" The marshal didn't. He took the cigarette and walked off, leaving Bette without her prop. Somehow the show went on, but clearly, Miss Davis was not a happy camper.

Celene Kendall's opening monologue early in Charles's first run at the San Francisco Fairmont Hotel's Venetian Room in 1984 was interrupted when a front row smoker blew a bug puff of smoke toward the stage. "**Darling, I wish you'd <u>in</u>hale. We're not electing a gay pope just yet.**"

One dark and stormy night during the last of his truly final (eighth) "Annual Final Farewell Performance" shows in 1990 at Pasadena Playhouse, Charles was performing a musical number that composer Billy Barnes had written for him, called "Doin' The Bette Davis." It was all about pursing your lips, bugging your eyes, twirling your arms, and sashaying across stage. Pianist Michael Ashton stopped playing at a regular break in the song, and while Charles was pantomiming the Davis arm twirl, a huge thunderclap shook the theatre. As if part of the act, Charles turned to the startled audience and abruptly ad-libbed "**Joan Crawford just farted!**"

The evening prompted one of those mysterious show-biz oddities: for years after that final engagement at Pasadena Playhouse's Balcony Theatre (capacity 150), Charles had easily that many or more fans claim they were there on that thunderclap/"Joan farted" night. It became legendary.

On one of the last nights of his final Pasadena engagement, just as Charles was doing his bit about *The Star* with "**Who the fuck is Barbara Lawrence?**," a voice from the back of the audience called out, "She's here!" And sure enough, there was Barbara Lawrence herself, looking very glamorous at 60-ish. She had been brought to the show by a friend who heard Charles's reference to her earlier in the run. So Charles immediately brought the gracious Barbara on stage, and continued his quips as Bette with the actual Ms. Lawrence. Another legendary night.

Having gotten his start in show business after graduating from Pasadena Playhouse in 1948, Charles considered his last-ever performance run there in 1990 an appropriate, "full circle" end to his career.

He seldom got serious on stage, preferring to maintain the show's high level of hilarity. But when Charles knew he had an audience exactly where he wanted them, as during those final shows, he would do a dramatic scene like Kate Hepburn's "Always Mademoiselle" from *Coco*, or the Bette Davis scene from *All About Eve* when Margo was stranded in the snowbound car with Celeste Holm. ("**Celestial Home**," he once ad-libbed, then quipped, "**Sounds like a gay senior center.**")

Charles Pierce, **Male Actress**, would sit down – a rarity on stage – then pantomime Bette changing the car's radio stations, adjusting the rearview mirror to check her makeup, and commenting on how strange it may seem for her to have a microphone or a cocktail in the car.

He asked for the lights to be lowered to a pin-spot on his face ("**I bring my own lighting designer everywhere I go. Don't you?**"), and requested that the pianist ("**Doesn't everyone have one in their back seat?**") play "Liebestraum." He did.

The chuckling stopped and once a more somber mood was established, Charles Pierce would perform Margo Channing's serious and self-introspective monologue about working women, authored by *All About Eve*'s brilliant writer/director Joseph L. Mankiewicz.

Funny business, a woman's career...
the things you drop on your way up the ladder,
so you can move faster.
You forget you'll need them again
when you get back to being a woman.

That's one career all females have in common,
whether we like it or not: being a woman.

Sooner or later we've all got to work at it,
no matter what other careers we've had.
Or wanted.

Nothing is any good unless you can look up
just before dinner, or turn around in bed,
and there he is.

Without that, you're not a woman.
You're something with a French provincial office
or a book full of clippings.

But you're not a woman....

Slow curtain. The end.

Slow fade-out. The end.

Thunderous applause.

CHARLES   PASADENA
PIERCE AT THE PLAYHOUSE

Pasadena Playhouse program from Charles Pierce's final engagement in 1990. Charles at age nine is dressed as Mae West (center), surrounded by his ladies (counter-clockwise from top left): Bette Davis, Gloria Swanson / Norma Desmond, Tallulah Bankhead, and Mae West. Program Design / Layout by Kirk Frederick.

Charles as Jeanette MacDonald, 1972

CHAPTER 6

THE FINALE(S)

The closing number of almost every Charles Pierce show, starting in the 1960s at The Gilded Cage, through the late '70s, was his aforementioned lip-synced, fully costumed, extravagantly over-produced rendition of Jeanette MacDonald's "San Francisco," the famed song from the movie of the same name.

The first few notes of the recording's intro would blast out over a showroom's sound system, and the crowd went wild.

Then Charles would appear in an outlandish replica of Jeanette's frock – all frilly fabrics, acres of flowery netting, puffy sleeves, and floor-length hoop skirts – plus the traditional MacDonald red curly wig and bonnet. He would camp it up while pantomiming the first few verses and chorus of the iconic song, encouraging the audience to sing along ("*San Francisco, open your Golden Gate…*"), which the fanatical followers, especially in San Francisco, were eager to do.

At the final orchestral break in the music, a long swing would lower out of the rafters, its ropes lined solidly with artificial flowers and blinking Christmas tree lights. Again, the crowd went ballistic. As the music built, Charles turned into an circus trapeze artist, swinging out over the cheering audience, prompting further hysteria. It was one of the most thrilling finales of a cabaret act, and it never failed to elicit a standing, screaming ovation as he exited.

After the number, he would make another quick change, but always wait for the ovations to build until he returned for the first of several (sometimes four or five) finale bows. On cue, one of the staff often presented him a huge bouquet of flowers, as if it were opening night. Charles would proceed to toss every single flower into the crowd. He tried to make sure that everyone got one.

The cheering would continue long enough for him to change into yet another glamour outfit and elegant blonde wig. Celene Kendall would make one final appearance. "**On behalf of the entire cast, which just happens to be me**," would begin more riotously funny material, often at the expense of victims in the front row: about a zaftig grand dame in a tight-fitting muumuu: "**I love to watch her laugh; so much of her is having a good time.**" ["**Write that down!**"] If there were two mixed couples near the stage, Celene deadpanned, "**The two guys are together; the gals are here as their lookouts.**"

"**And look at this happy couple. Why, it's the Hydes, ladies and gentlemen: Naugha and his lovely wife Formalda. And over there: please say hello to the Rhea sisters: Gonna, Diah, and Pyah. And here we have the Andrews Sisters: See No Evil, Speak No Evil, and Laverne.**"

In the smaller nightclubs, there always seemed to be someone in the front row who put a foot or two up on the stage's edge by the end of the show. "**Are you in show business?**," Charles would ask the hapless, unsuspecting fan, who usually said 'no.' "**Then take your friggin' feet off my stage**," Charles would snark, with a wink and a smirk.

"**Famous last lines? From the Titanic captain: 'Let's have a party; stop for ice.'**

"**Or from Isadora Duncan's sister: 'Wear the green scarf. It'll bring out your eyes.'**

"**Or Jayne Mansfield: 'Duck!'**

"**Or Marie Antoinette: 'Ok, fellas, knock it off.'**"

"**I need a drink. But bartender, please: just a child's portion of vodka this time.**

"**We might be here for quite some time…. Till Whoopi Goldberg can run a comb through her hair. Till Angie Dickinson combs hers. Or till Shelley Winters does a 'Weight Watchers' commercial.**

"**Shelley Winters!? She's designed her own clothing line for the plus-size girl; the logo is an elephant! By the way, how do you have sex with Shelley Winters? You roll her in flour and look for the wet spot. Poor Shelley Winters! She came to a party I gave once, in a silver sequined gown, and she twirled. We all went blind!**"

"**What does** [then First Lady] **Barbara Bush do with all of her old clothes? She wears them.**

"**Why do moths have such small balls? Very few of them know how to dance.**

"**Does Lucille Ball? Can Buddy Hackett? Does William Bendix? Was Marvin Gaye? Does Tom Cruise?**"

When his older fans would express disappointment about Charles no longer doing his Jeanette MacDonald "San Francisco" finale, he would explain why, then appease them with a favorite old San Francisco story.

"**An elegantly fey older gentleman was sitting in the bar at the St. Francis Hotel in April 1906, and in a very lispy voice, asked the bartender if he could have a Singapore Sling** [with the most sibilant-possible hissing of 's's]. **The bartender told him that they didn't serve his 'kind,' so, no: no drink. Our little friend got very indignant, and said 'Listen dearie, my money is good, and I'm just parched, so please** [more hissing], **I want a drink.' The bartender stood his ground and said 'I guess you didn't hear me; I said we don't serve your kind here, so you'll have to leave.' Just then the earthquake hit. Things crashed all around our little gent, but he sat there untouched as the bartender crawled up out of the rubble. 'So there, dearie,' said our little friend. 'Now do I get my drink or do I have Her do it again?'**"

"**I was in the rest room here at the club before the show, and noticed a sign on the wall reading 'Employees must wash hands before returning to the other employees.'**

"**Someone wrote on the stall wall: 'My mother made me a homosexual.' Under it, someone else scrawled: 'If I send her some yarn, will she make me one too?'**"

"**I was on an international tour, playing the smart supper clubs of Jamaica, and before I got into costume one night, I had to use the men's room. Standing at the urinal next to me was a very attractive local, who smiled at me. I couldn't help glancing down at his ample appendage, which had the name WENDY tattooed on it. I asked him if that was the name of his girlfriend. 'Well, no,' he replied proudly. 'When I get excited, it actually reads WELCOME TO JAMAICA. NOW HAVE A NICE DAY.'**"

Charles often quoted Noël Coward's line about having just "a talent to amuse." Like so many entertainers, including Sir Noël, Charles also had a need to please, and of course to elicit laughter and applause.

His Mae allowed him to show off his flirtatious, sexy side. Kate Hepburn permitted him to be dramatic and reveal his acting chops. Bette Davis gave him alcohol-induced authority to be bitchy and say almost anything he wanted, politically correct or not.

His gay-oriented humor in the pre-HIV/AIDS '60s and '70s was often raunchy, with deliberate innuendo and a liberating sense of sexy playfulness on stage and off. Audiences responded in kind. He took that home with him, but nothing and no one else. He was always alone; always mademoiselle. There was the occasional trick or treat, but it was most often followed by regret or disappointment.

Charles was married to his career, and in the years I knew him, he never connected with anyone for a long-term relationship. I'm not sure he really wanted to. When guys did go home with him, they often asked him to do Bette Davis or dress as Mae West. They loved the persona, not the person. Charles saw through that every time.

It sometimes made him lonesome, but never lonely. He had his movies, his record albums, his fantasies, his "ladies," and his extraordinary ability to write witty banter for them. He did constant research to make characters his own alter egos. He got lost in them. But none of them, including the real him, had any personal life to speak of. At least it was not spoken of on stage. Or, for that matter, off.

In my 20 years working with him, easy-going Charles did not lose his temper. Well, maybe once....

Between his regular engagements in the early 1980s at Studio One's Backlot in West Hollywood when he lived in Southern California, Charles would accept short gigs in nearby gay-friendly areas like Palm Springs, easily drivable from his North Hollywood home. His agent Budd Haas once booked him for one performance near San Diego's gay area, at a new nightclub, formerly a Chinese restaurant.

The place was still painted white, with fluorescent lighting, an asbestos ceiling, folding chairs, and a short, eight-foot-square platform that served as the stage in the far corner of a low-ceilinged room. There was no "backstage" access. Charles had to enter through the audience from the opposite end of the building, out of a storage closet, which served as his dressing room and makeup area. He could not do his usual quick costume changes off stage, so he reverted to his original Florida routine of wearing one basic outfit, then stepping behind a folding screen (with no one there to help him) to change wigs, voices, props, and accessories, all the while narrating the show over a microphone behind the screen.

That worked adequately until the finale, which he had promised the owner would be his popular Bette/Tallulah bitch fight (no space for Jeanette and her swing this time). To do it right, Charles felt, he needed to change into the basic black satin *All About Eve* costume, wig, and makeup. So there was no choice; he had to be escorted through the crowded room for the final change. We alerted a few waiters to help create a path so he could get through the audience quickly, back to his dressing closet to change, then return to the small stage.

After he did an abbreviated but brilliantly funny version of the Bette/Tallulah back-and-forth, he bid the rowdy, rambunctious audience good night. He introduced me, and I slid along a side wall to take my quick farewell bow on stage, then took his hand to help get him out through the crowded room once again. As we pushed our way through, one of the drunks lunged in front of him and blurted out: "Charles, you really should wear gloves; your hands look so old."

That did it. Those big baby blues saw red, his face got flushed and puffy, and I swear that if Charles had claws, he would have drawn blood from the guy. Charles bristled and added a couple inches to his already imposing six-foot height, spitting out the only nasty invective hurled directly at an audience member that I ever heard from him:

"**How DARE you speak to me like that, you son of a bitch**," he growled, with a look that should have withered the guy. It may have. We'll never know.

Charles turned to me and said "**Let's get out of here**." We plowed through the crowd, slammed the closet door behind us, and started packing. He got out of costume and makeup, and changed clothes as fast as I loaded the car through a back door. We left ten minutes later and drove directly to the nearby freeway entrance north to Los Angeles.

The incident was not spoken of again. And he never wore gloves.

: : : : :

Charles attracted celebrities, especially the urbane, open-minded ones who liked to laugh. When she first "toured" San Francisco in *Mame*, Angela Lansbury saw him at The Gilded Cage, and again whenever his and her shows played San Francisco concurrently. When Bea Arthur and Charles became close friends later in their lives (long after "Maude" and "Golden Girls"), Bea invited Angela (her pal from *Mame*) to her home for

Charles Pierce, Angela Lansbury, and Bea Arthur at Bea's home, c. 1990

an intimate dinner with Charles. Angela reminded him how much she had enjoyed his take-off of *Mame* at The Gilded Cage in the 1960s, and how it was one of her most cherished and vivid memories.

Lauren ("That's 'Betty' to you, Chaz") Bacall and her pals in the touring production of *Woman of the Year* joined Harvey Fierstein and the local cast of *Beyond the Fringe* in booths of San Francisco's Plush Room cabaret in the Hotel York. After the show, Betty and her entourage met Charles at a nearby gay bar, the New Bell Saloon, where the popular local musical prodigy David Kelsey held court at a large pipe organ with several keyboards. David saw Bacall enter the room, stopped his act, graciously acknowledged and announced her presence, then launched into the musical theme from *Murder on the Orient Express*. She was elated at the recognition. And the standing ovation.

Between that and her exuberance over Charles's performance that night, The Great Bacall bought everyone in the bar a drink. Her friend and co-performer in *WOTY*, Michael Laughlin (the same guy who, coincidentally, years later became my life partner and close to Charles) was there and later admitted that Betty was so frugal – not the actual word he used – that he had never seen her buy even one drink for anyone when they went out together after *Woman of the Year* performances.

Charles Pierce fans also included Barbara Cook, Margaret Whiting, Rita Moreno, Eartha Kitt, Maxene Andrews, Sharon McNight, Michael Feinstein, Nancy LaMott, Wesla Whitfield, Ruth Hastings, Craig Jessup, Val Diamond, David Reign, and every other major cabaret entertainer who played San Francisco's beloved and beautiful "Tush Room of the Hotel Yuck," as Charles dubbed it in jest.

And every time, at the end of every show, Charles would graciously introduce each celebrity, and as hard as it was for him to give up the follow-spot, he always shared it with his fans out there in the dark. They loved him for it, and most came backstage afterward, always effusive in their praise.

Michael Feinstein loved Charles so much, he actually told him that if he ever needed a pianist at the last minute, Michael would gladly oblige. Be careful what you offer; not long after, Charles's Studio One pianist had an emergency and sure enough, Mr. Feinstein was there, and played the show as if he had been doing it for years.

In the early '70s, we once held the starting time of Charles's late show at San Francisco's Gold Street so Bette Midler and Barry Manilow could get there after their premiere Bay Area performance in Berkeley across the Bay. They came, they saw, they convulsed; we all went out for ice cream and giggles after the show, then the Divine Miss M invited us to her show the next night at the Berkeley Community Theatre. We were driven in a stretch limo across the Bay Bridge for one of those history-making, memorable nights in show business. Charles was in awe of Midler and Manilow. We all were.

It was not easy for Charles to praise other entertainers. Call it professional jealousy. Call it ego. Call it rude. But Charles sat transfixed and drop-jawed during Midler's performance. It may have helped that she introduced him at the end of her show, and told the audience that they MUST go see him at Gold Street. It's impossible to know if her endorsement had anything to do with it, but the rest of that month-long Gold Street run was completely sold out.

During Bette's show, we sat next to Carol Channing. We were all escorted backstage afterward to meet Miss M again, who, teeny at under five feet, looked up at Carol and Charles and uttered something funny about being between two "towering" comedy talents.

Strangely, Carol Channing was the only star Charles ever "did" on stage who actually saw and loved his show, also at Gold Street, and several times later in his career. Carol once made Charles laugh out loud when he introduced her from the stage at Gold Street, and she stood up to say that *he* did her better than *she* did. It was one of the very few times the audience (or I) ever saw Charles Pierce actually get tears in his eyes.

This was never supposed to be divulged, but someone did sneak Bette Davis into the Studio One Backlot one night in the late '70s. Charles didn't know she was there, and he did a particularly raunchy and not-very-flattering Bette that night. When I went out after the show to invite her backstage to surprise Charles, she snapped at me: "There is only one female impersonator who does me right, and his name is Arthur Blake. No thank you, I'll pass." Charles never knew, although he (out of drag) was introduced to her at a private event shortly thereafter when their mutual friend Geraldine Fitzgerald (Charles called her "Geraldine Fitzgeraldine" in his act) brought Ms. Davis along. Bette brushed Charles off with the same dismissive words about Mr. Blake, but never mentioned the show.

In addition to Ms. Lansbury, Charles's Gilded Cage audiences in those six years of the '60s had also included Rudolf Nureyev, Dame Margot Fonteyn, Hermione Gingold, Richard Deacon, Leslie Uggams, Della Reese, Anne Francine, Tammy Grimes, and Gale Gordon.

Over five San Francisco summers from 1984 to 1988, Charles packed the grand Venetian Room (**"formerly the men's room at the Vatican"**) of Nob Hill's Fairmont Hotel two shows a night, six nights a week, for several weeks each season. Among the fans (600 at each show) were Tina Turner and Vicki Carr, who stayed in San Francisco after their respective shows closed there on Sunday night to see Charles's Tuesday night opening. Rock Hudson showed up with Armistead Maupin and the NFL's Dave Kopay. Dixie Carter and Hal Holbrook came, as did Richard Chamberlain, Dom DeLuise, the mayor, governor, senators, assembly-men and -women, local society types, columnists, entertainers, television stars, and every wealthy "A-gay" (or wannabe) north of San José and south of Sonoma/Napa.

This was one of those engagements that Charles had dreamed of: possibly the most prestigious supper club in San Francisco, if not all of California, with the estimable Dick Bright Orchestra, proper sound and light systems with knowledgeable staff to operate them, gourmet food and comfortably elegant dining accommodations for the discerning audience.

But there was no backstage area. Charles got dressed and made-up in his sixth-floor suite, then took a service elevator down to the kitchen, through the dish-washing area to access his waiter-station area for changes and entrances. The smell was overpowering, even in the service elevator, so Charles brought his '30s perfume atomizer filled with Shalimar, and sprayed the elevator each time he rode it. We chuckled over the pun of his introduction: "*Mister* Charles Pierce."

After the show on the first night Dixie and Hal came to the Fairmont, they came up to the Charles's dressing room suite. He was still getting out of makeup, so he asked me to offer drinks to his friends. Dixie pulled me aside and said, "Just give me a straight vodka on the rocks in a water glass. Don't tell Hal." After I handed her the glass, Hal took me by the arm, walked me over to the bar, and said, "Just give me a straight vodka on the rocks in a water glass. Don't tell Dixie." I wondered if this was a routine they did at every party (before they both quit drinking). It was funny. So were they.

Dixie Carter became one of Charles's close friends and ardent admirers, and was partly responsible for getting him a guest-star appearance on an episode of "Designing Women." He played a cruise ship waiter who doubled as the onboard entertainment, giving him yet another opportunity to do his Bette Davis routine on TV. Dixie once told me that Charles had probably the best comic timing of any entertainer she knew. Hal was equally in awe of him, and said so. Often.

Charles Pierce engagements in New York City were also star-studded. Ingrid Bergman snuck in unnoticed to catch his raucous Village Gate show, then came backstage to invite us as her guests at the next day's matinée of *The Constant Wife* on Broadway.

Anthony Hopkins jumped in a cab after his performance in *Equus* to enjoy Charles's late show, then invited us the next afternoon to be his guest in the on-stage seats during the play. Charles wasn't up for it, but I went. Mr. (then; since Sir) Hopkins and I dined afterward at Barrymore's. He raved about Charles, and told me stories of his terrifyingly nervous early scenes with Katharine Hepburn in *The Lion in Winter*, his very first film.

Sandy Duncan came with Tommy Tune. He was an old friend of the *Geese* producers Phil Oesterman and Jim Sink, who also produced Charles at The Village Gate. Tommy loved Charles so much, they did a show together, and appeared later in fund-raising benefits during the '80s. Charles was not always happy doing all those benefits for free, but he knew the cause; and if Tommy Tune asked, Charles was there.

Maxwell Caulfield showed up at the Charles Pierce Show with Juliet Mills. So did Joan Blondell, Hermione Gingold, Mel Tormé, Rip Taylor, Chita Rivera, Dr. Ruth Westheimer, Claudette Colbert, and Diana Rigg. Lucille Ball and Vivian Vance were there, along with legendary Broadway stars like Carol Lawrence, Patti LuPone, and Bernadette Peters, usually with new "CP virgins," at some of New York's finest nightclubs: The Village Gate, Les Mouches, Freddy's Supper Club, and The Ballroom.

Again, the stars came backstage after the finale, and there were often pictures the next day in several New York daily newspapers acknowledging the backstage celebrity meetings with the "cross-over" diva of drag.

When Charles did the last-ever nightclub engagement at famed Ciro's on Sunset Boulevard in late 1971 and early 1972 (before it later became The Comedy Store), John Gielgud was in the audience, amused and flattered that Charles used an ahead-of-its-time line he had heard John say in David Storey's Broadway play called *Home*: "If a person can't be what they are, what's the point of being anything at all?" John (later dubbed Sir) came backstage at Ciro's to gush.

So did Martha Raye. And Kaye Ballard. And the young actor Michael Kearns. Michael Bennett was in L.A. doing *A Chorus Line*; he brought his new wife Donna McKechnie and the rest of his cast to the show at Ciro's, then threw an after-Charles party at their rented Hollywood Hills mansion. It was the most relaxed I had seen Charles, partly because he was the center of attention, and partly because he was surrounded in the hot tub by several attractive, young, adoring (mostly male) cast members.

In the mid-'70s, Studio One's Backlot became *the* Los Angeles nightclub, in the heart of West Hollywood. Charles dubbed it "Baja Beverly Hills" and enjoyed working the intimate 200-seat cabaret upstairs from the popular gay disco. The Backlot had a separate entrance, up a long fire escape staircase in back of the building. The stars waited in line on the stairs with everyone else. Ann-Margret was there. Paul Lynde, Charles Nelson Reilly, Vincent Price, Julie Harris, Betty Garrett, Kim Darby, Ed Begley Jr., and Johnny Ray all waited to get in. And they all came to Charles's dressing room after the show. There were always photos and lots more laughter.

Ann-Margret and husband/producer Roger Smith rushed backstage to ask Charles if he would "open" her show at Caesars Palace in October 1978. "**YES!**," Charles gushed, almost before they had finished asking. Ann-Margret and Roger invited us to their Malibu home a few weeks later for an afternoon of volleyball and barbecue, and we talked specifics of the upcoming show, her first in years since the Tahoe accident that nearly killed her when she fell from a backstage device.

Charles did his best to warm up, woo, and win over the unfamiliar Las Vegas crowd doing a 15-minute version of his act: the Living Dolls ("Moppettes," he called them till Jim Henson dubbed his the "Muppets," then they became Pierce's Puppet People, and later the Living Dolls): three-foot-high doll bodies strapped around his neck. Charles wore appropriate wigs and all black, maneuvering the arms and legs of the dolls while mouthing words to pre-recorded songs, bringing the dolls hysterically to life on a table in front of him: Shirley Temple, Dolly Parton, the Singing Nun, and Bette Davis, who after a minute, became a live, full-body version through the magic of break-away costumes and tricky but effective lighting by the brilliant Broadway designer Ken Billington. Charles did his best, but the crowd was there to see Ann-Margret, not a guy in a dress wearing doll bodies and camping it up as Bette Davis. The response was civil but tepid.

He played to over 1,200 people at each of the 28 shows he "opened" for Ann-Margret over 14 consecutive days. Joan Rivers was the first celebrity to come backstage, appearing at the door like a dowdy miniature matron in a turban. She introduced herself as if Charles didn't remember that earlier that year she had directed the movie *Rabbit Test*, in which he

Charles with Joan Rivers in *Rabbit Test*, 1978

had played the Queen of England. Joan raved about his Caesars show, and threatened (jokingly?) to "borrow" some of his material.

There is still debate about who stole the line "**Liz Taylor saw a sign that said 'Wet Floor,' so she did**" from whom. (Charles used it at Caesars in 1978; Joan said it on TV in 1982 about a football player). Or when Liz got plump, who came up with "**What do you buy Liz Taylor for her birthday? Stretch jewelry!**"? Joan used some of his material for years. She once admitted publicly (and often privately) that she had been very much influenced by Charles.

He did come up with this routine about Ms. Taylor, as Bette Davis: "**Liz used to be pretty. Pretty, pretty, pretty. Now she's pretty fat** [gesturing on "fat" with his index finger tapping the ash off Bette's cigarette]. **Liz went to a fat farm and lost 40 pounds: all mascara! 'Liz,' I said to her: 'you know you're fat when the crotch on your caftan is tight!' Remember when we all wanted to look like Elizabeth Taylor, and now we do?**"

One of the few Caesars performances Charles did enjoy (perhaps the only one) was the night that his dear friend Shelley Werk flew from San Francisco to see him in Las Vegas. She had been in the front row at Gold Street years before, and was laughing so much that Charles stopped the show to ask her name. "Kitty," she replied. "**Kitty what?**," he asked. Without a pause, she said "Litter." During the laugh, Charles-as-Bette took a long drag on his cigarette, looked down at Shelley, and dead-panned yet another of his quick and witty ad-libs: "**No shit!**" They remained friends for life.

Shelley brought her friend, singer Val Diamond with her to Caesars in '78. A few months later Val joined *Beach Blanket Babylon* in San Francisco, which Shelley was also in. Val was featured in the show for almost 30 years, still on the record books. Charles was a huge fan of Val's, a rarity for him.

Charles didn't have much fun in Las Vegas. Playing Caesars Palace was a big cross-over career step and good for his résumé, but except for Joan Rivers and a few old friends and fans (including Liberace), the Vegas crowd wasn't really with him, especially in the cavernous Caesars showroom. He was used to smaller, more intimate cabaret rooms and audiences. It was an honor for him to work with Ann-Margret, and she and her team could not have been nicer, more receptive, or more supportive. But Charles was not a Vegas headliner, and in spite of the glamorous gig, he was better and more comfortable when he was the star of the show, in smaller venues.

His saddest finale was at an odd nightclub in San Francisco called "Olympus: America's First Bi-Sex Showplace." As a favor to the owner, Charles agreed to open the club in late 1974, along with the budding *Beach Blanket Babylon*, which had just done a successful but limited engagement at the nearby Savoy Tivoli in North Beach. There were three shows a night at Olympus. On alternate evenings, Charles would do the first and third shows with *BBB* between them, and the next night Charles would perform between two *BBB* shows: a confusing schedule at best.

As funny and popular as Charles was, he was no match for the raucous glitz of *BBB*, with its cast of 10, orchestra of five guys in poodle outfits, shimmering sets, extravagant costumes, and ceiling-high hats. So whether Charles opened for *BBB* or vice versa, he did not get the response he was used to, and asked to opt out of his contract after just a few weeks. The last show he did there was the hardest night he had ever been through, except perhaps for one night at Caesars Palace, when he got NO laughs, prompting another ad-lib: "**This is an English-speaking audience, isn't it?**" We DID write that one down, but Charles rarely needed to use it again.

Olympus was not a satisfying finale to his San Francisco years. Shortly thereafter Charles moved back to Los Angeles, and started a whole new phase of his career in the late '70s and '80s, making occasional trips back to S.F. to appear at his two other favorite nightclubs there (after The Gilded Cage and Gold Street): the Plush Room and the Venetian Room.

It was during these years that Charles developed the finale he would use to close every performance the remainder of his career: his live rendition of Marlene Dietrich's song "Illusions." He played it straight: no bad German accent and no campy pronunciations of her 'L's and 'R's. He used his smooth baritone voice in a comfortable key, accompanied by his live pianist – usually the gifted Joan Edgar wearing a tuxedo "to further the cross-dressing," he quipped – in a tellingly accurate performance of the song about life and show business being a series of illusions (*"slightly used, second hand"*) like his cabaret act (*"light as air, built on sand"*). It summarized his stage persona and his entire act: illusions he created of bigger-than-life celebrity women. And what light fun it had all been.

Ironically, Olympus closed its doors forever shortly after Charles left it in 1974, and *Beach Blanket Babylon* found its new home six months later, opening at nearby Fugazi Hall in North Beach for "six weeks only."

The show at the renamed Club Fugazi celebrated its 40th anniversary (of its opening there) on June 27, 2015, having gained the distinction as the longest-running cabaret show in history.

In 1994, *Beach Blanket Babylon* producer and pal Steve Silver invited Charles to appear at the grand 20th anniversary celebration of Steve's by-then-legendary *BBB*, performed by many returning cast members (including me, the original Fugazi M&M Peanut, Tumbling Tumbleweed, and Tap-Dancing Christmas Tree) for one night only in May at the San Francisco Opera House.

Because Charles felt he had helped launch *BBB* twenty years earlier by sharing "his" 1974 engagement at Olympus with Steve's fledgling show, he came out of retirement to appear one last time as Bette Davis, in the grandeur of the Opera House.

Just before Charles went on, Steve came into his dressing room to ask if Charles could shorten his routine. Partly because of the cheers, applause, ovations, and laughter, the show was running long.

Always the agreeable one, Charles said that of course he would. He went on stage, and after just ten minutes of the funniest, best Bette ever – reminiscent of his 1974 and 1982 "big house" triumphs at the Dorothy Chandler Pavilion – he came up with one of the funniest, most spontaneous and appropriate ad-libs he had ever done, referring to his brief appearance:

"Steve Silver asked me to come out of retirement – I actually call it my 'abdication' – and return to San Francisco for a special cameo appearance here tonight. Well, ladies and gentlemen, this has been more like a broach."

Charles said good night and good-bye, and got a thunderous ovation, which ironically added another few minutes to the evening.

That time we didn't need to "**write that down**." Except for a brief appearance in a New York Town Hall benefit the following month, this May 1994 appearance – almost 40 years after his very first professional engagement – was the last time Charles performed on stage: in front of his largest single audience of 3,200 adoring fans and admirers, at the most opulent "showroom" he had ever played.

Finally: a fitting finale.

Charles as Bette Davis in his last appearance at the San Francisco Opera House, 1994

Charles as Margo Channing in *Applause*,
Kimo Productions, San Francisco, 1974

CHAPTER 7

APPLAUSE

pplause, applause, applause. Charles Pierce audiences went wild, in intimate nightclubs and grand opera houses. His critics went overboard with praise in their reviews. Unanimously. But he had studied to be an actor, and he wanted to act in live theatre.

On Broadway even.

In fact, we were so sure that his show would be a hit on Broadway, we decided to try selling a theatrical idea to a New York producer we knew. The elegant old Ritz Theatre (now the Walter Kerr on 48th St.) was vacant at the time, so Charles and I flew to New York on November 1, 1988, to pitch our idea for *Charles at The Ritz* (possibly endorsed by famed perfumer Charles of The Ritz). So we flew out of San Francisco for a few days in New York.

But at the exact moment our plane touched down at JFK airport, the huge Loma Prieta earthquake hit San Francisco, where our producer friend had a show preparing to open the following week. The theatre was damaged, and his show was delayed. So our meeting – and *Charles At The Ritz* on Broadway – never happened.

Fortunately, *Applause*, the Tony Award-winning Broadway musical, *had been* produced for Charles in 1974, in San Francisco. Kimo Cochran, an old friend, fan, and supporter, was owner of the popular and long-lived Kimo's bar and cabaret on California and Polk Streets. He wanted to produce another of his Kimo Productions: local musicals, which had featured all-male casts in shows like *Dames at Sea* and *Hello, Dolly!*.

This time Kimo wanted Charles to play Margo Channing in *Applause*, the musical based on *All About Eve*. (The 1950 movie starring Bette Davis as Margo Channing had been made into the 1970 Broadway musical version for Lauren Bacall.) But rights were not granted to Kimo; apparently the publishers did not want a man playing Margo, even though this time, the rest of the cast in the production of *Applause* would have men playing men, and women playing women.

As luck and timing would have it, Carol Channing heard about the problem with the *Applause* rights. Coincidentally, she had recently seen Charles at Gold Street, so Miss Channing invited her friends Betty Comden and Adolph Green, who wrote the book for *Applause*, to attend his show with her in San Francisco. After they roared with laughter over the Bette/ Tallulah bitch fight, Comden and Green rushed backstage to say they were calling the *Applause* publishers the next day, to insist they give the okay for Charles to play Margo. "Perfect casting," they said.

Done.

Well, not so fast. Kimo had limited resources, and chose the ornate old (but rarely used) California Hall on lower Polk Street in which to present the show. It had once been a "union house," so the local musicians' union tried to require that he hire 16 players. Kimo said no; he would do the show with a high-school band before he would be forced to engage expensive union musicians in this small local show, especially considering that once one union was involved, he would also be required to hire union stagehands, performers, and house staff. He could not afford that.

So Kimo discussed the issue with Charles. They agreed to do a non-union production. Charles ignored his own nightclub performers' union rules, and did the show anyway; he paid a fine and was banished by the union for a few years. He didn't care.

Kimo hired the gifted Michael Biagi, a prodigy who had played piano for some of Charles's engagements in San Francisco. (Michael later served as pianist, musical director, and conductor for Charles's encore Dorothy Chandler Pavilion concert in 1982, and for several of Charles's subsequent nightclub engagements, as well as for Tommy Tune later in their careers.) Michael had been musical director and conductor for an orchestra of young musicians that had just done *Applause* in the East Bay area; Kimo engaged Mr. Biagi and his orchestra, agreeing to pay a stipend for transportation costs into San Francisco for their rehearsals and performances.

Charles and the cast walked into the cavernous California Hall (a meeting space that looked – and sounded – like a basketball court with no nets or lines on the floor) for the first orchestra rehearsal a week before opening night. After Biagi led the talented band of teenagers through the bouncy overture, the entire place erupted in cheers and applause. It was Broadway-quality brilliant.

Charles said something silly about not really wanting to work in a "Hall," so they changed the name temporarily to California Theatre. It worked, and so did the production. Charles carried the show through rehearsals in the Hall/Theatre – echoing acoustics, bad sound system, flimsy sets and all – but the production elements reeked of cheap community theatre. A few days before opening, they brought in Margo's costumes and wigs, which were not up to Charles's standards. So he called in his trusty friends to do the impossible: create 20 different costumes (mostly from Charles's storage units) and wigs, and please do SOMETHING with the sets. They/we all did. In just three days.

"A Jazzy, Vibrant Show" was the headline of a glowing review in the *San Francisco Chronicle*. All but one of about 30 other critics raved, mostly about Charles. He was the talk and toast of the town. Audiences loved it, and ultimately the under-rehearsed show found its legs. Choreographer Jean Martin did wonders with the youthful cast of dancers. The supporting cast was strong, especially young Tony Michaels as the gay hairdresser Duane, who left the camping-it-up to Charles-as-Margo, plus a bit of Bette. Even the show's original Broadway director Ron Field saw the production and gushed that "Charles IS Margo."

Applause was one of only two theatrical ventures Charles attempted after his early career as a stand-up comic had developed through the late 1950s and into the '60s. The other production had been *Geese*.

Later in life, when Charles was asked if he had any regrets, he said he wished he had done Broadway. (However, he joked dismissively that he could never do Shakespeare after he read the stage direction "**Lady Macbeth enters with candle upper center.**" [Wait for it.]) He did play two sold-out benefits at Broadway's Beacon Theatre. He had appeared with vaudeville fan dancer Sally Rand at the Dorothy Chandler Pavilion, and with Hildegarde at Carnegie Hall. He also felt he had really "made it" by playing The Venetian Room and Freddy's.

Throughout five successful summer engagements in the mid-'80s at the elegant Venetian Room in San Francisco's Fairmont Hotel, Charles did two shows a night, six nights a week, for as many as 12 weeks at a time, with basically the same show: Blondes, Mae, Kate, sometimes Joan Collins, Bette and Tallulah and Joan Crawford, Finale.

Depending on the Fairmont audience size (usually sold out at 600) and the demographic mixture of society darlings, celebrities, avid fans, young hunks, and old drunks, Charles would wing it. New comedy material started flowing so fast that we reverted to videotaping every show, as we had in the early '70s when he was perfecting his revised solo act after *Geese*. Charles would watch tapes of particularly good shows and add any new material into his regular routines.

We saved those old VHS tapes, along with recordings of his many appearances on major TV talk shows (hosted by the likes of Merv Griffin, Mike Douglas, Regis Philbin) promoting his engagements over the years, and of his guest appearances in and out of drag on TV shows as varied as "Love, American Style" (1972), "Chico and The Man" ('76), "Starsky and Hutch" ('77), "Wonder Woman" ('78), "Laverne and Shirley" ('80), "Fame" ('83), and "Designing Women" ('87).

After Dick Cavett's TV interviews with Bette Davis, Mae West, and Katharine Hepburn in the 1970s, fans of Charles Pierce urged Cavett to interview one of the great impressionists of these legendary ladies as well. Cavett did just that in 1981, and it was a *tour de force* performance for both of them: Charles as Kate, Bette, and Crawford, and Dick as himself, who clearly had no idea what to expect (he had neither seen nor heard of Charles). Cavett tried to interview Charles-as-Kate as if it were actually Ms. Hepburn. It didn't work.

Following that first segment of the interview show, when Charles went offstage to change into his Bette outfit, Dick looked into the camera, rolled his eyes, and feigned fainting. After the commercial break, he introduced Bette. Charles did the *All About Eve* "woman's career" speech; Cavett was smitten. That episode of the Cavett show became enormously popular.

Another of the many TV appearances Charles made to promote his shows came as he began his 25th anniversary in show-biz with the first of ten major engagements at San Francisco's newest nightclub, the posh Plush Room at the Hotel York. ABC-TV's local affiliate KGO Channel 7 employed a savvy young reporter named Paul Wynne, who was an avid

Charles Pierce fan, and asked if he could report "live from backstage" on the afternoon of the engagement's opening in 1980.

Normally Charles would not have allowed such an intimate, invasive interview, but Paul was such an important and appreciative critic that Charles acquiesced. It turned out to be one of the most quotable of any reports, and it certainly helped increase audiences. Paul started his live "7 On The Town" show by stating that "Charles Pierce is not really a 'female impersonator.' He's a stand-up nightclub comic, one of the toughest professions. He's a quick-change artist, a mimic, an actor, a movie historian, a clown, an illusionist, a man with a razor-sharp wit....

"He's a pioneer who made the Jim Baileys possible. His cabaret show is probably not for everyone. It's generally R- to X-rated, and he certainly gets more laughs per minute than any show I can remember."

Paul and Charles sat together in the dressing room at Charles's makeup table, and it was the closest that the public had ever been to the inner sanctum of backstage. They chatted amiably about the structure and content of the shows. The airing of the interview was interspersed with some of Charles's funniest lines and ad-libs from previous engagements.

When Paul joked that he would like to stay and watch Charles get made-up and dressed, Charles said no, he had to draw the line, and retain some of the mystique of show-biz. And anyway, Charles said, **"there's nothing more bizarre than a naked female impersonator."**

::::: :

Videotapes of Charles's shows offer rare footage and insight: there was never a typical, routine, or standard Charles Pierce show; no two were ever the same. He would switch lines around almost every performance. When a show was predictable, it wasn't fun or challenging for him. Spontaneous laughter is best, new material essential. And more fun.

There was always something new, something that sparked a departure from the routine. Something Mae would say while flirting with a front-row hottie. Something Kate would warble about her favorite roles. Something new that Bette would find to bitch about. And most shows would end with several minutes of introducing friends and celebrities (or both) in the audience, plus prolonged ad-libbing, inevitably accompanied by more laughter and applause.

Charles Pierce was almost impossible to define. The "female impersonator" label seemed to imply actually "impersonating" – embodying or personifying – the female in question. Costumed in a sparkling, form-fitting, floor-length gown, with a long feather boa, and an extravagantly coiffed blonde wig, he would strike a glamorous fashion-model pose and announce "**A 'female impersonator'? Me? Ha! Have you ever seen a woman *dressed* like this? Honey, it takes a <u>man</u> to wear an outfit like this.**"

Or "**I'm a gentleman dressed as a lady for financial purposes only. I make money the old-fashioned way: I *earn* it,**" which was his nod to the then-popular John Houseman TV commercials for Smith-Barney.

Charles took his entertainment form a step further. He did his comic impressions of female celebrities, so what he did was more accurately, if awkwardly, called "female impressionism." That sounded too much like an art form, so he kept trying to re-invent what to call himself, throughout almost his entire career.

When he was interviewed in 1976 for a newspaper article about his first appearance at Studio One's Backlot in West Hollywood, Charles was asked about how he got started, and what he liked to be called. "**Call me anything you like,**" he said, "**but not 'Charlie' or 'Chuck,' and never a 'female impersonator' or 'drag queen.' That's a man who pretends or believes he is a woman. If I spent an hour on stage trying to convince you I was female, I'd be an 'impersonator.' If anybody thinks I'm kidding anybody – that I think I really am Bette Davis – well, ha! No…**

"**The point of my act is having fun with the instantly identifiable characteristics of famous women. I depend on satire, exaggeration, and camp humor to communicate with an audience. I don't do the women the way they are off-screen or off-stage. I do my impressions of their over-the-top gestures or vocal foibles, saying things that I think would be fun for them to say, or my version of their famous lines done in a campy or exaggerated, unexpected way. Again, it's all about having fun.**"

Questions about how he got started seemed to rankle him, especially the more times he was asked about it for articles in newspapers and magazines that were supposed to be promoting upcoming local appearances. He would often gloss over his early years, preferring to focus on the current act. But two opportunities came along just before he retired, and he knew this was probably the right time to give his own account, for the "permanent record" as it were, about how he got his start in show biz.

Author Anthony Slide interviewed him for the Academy of Motion Picture Arts and Sciences (AMPAS) 1986 publication, *Great Pretenders, The Illustrated History of Male and Female Impersonation.* Three years later, Dallas's Southern Methodist University sent their History Department director Ronald L. Davis to Charles's North Hollywood home for a lengthy, thorough interview, which became part of SMU's Oral History Program.

Charles told both interviewers that by 1952, having graduated from the Pasadena Playhouse school of acting several years before, he realized that making a living as an actor was going to be a challenge, especially in roles where he could use his innate gifts as a comedian.

In 1953, he had gone to the Bar of Music nightclub in Hollywood to see Arthur Blake, the well-known impressionist who specialized in comic characterizations of over-the-top stars like Bette Davis and Tallulah Bankhead (remember that Blake was the only impersonator of Bette Davis that she actually approved of and tolerated).

Charles was impressed and intrigued with both the freedom and the glamour of Mr. Blake's presentation. In those early years of his act, he appeared in a tuxedo (later in gowns, but less successfully), with twin pianos playing behind him, often performing for movie stars in the audience.

"**I could do that**," Charles thought.

Charles had also been toying with funny ideas about "what if" situations, which he would experiment with at parties. What if Bette Davis had played Scarlett O'Hara? What if Eleanor Roosevelt did a nightclub act after she left the White House? What if Norma Desmond had gone to prison for killing her lover in *Sunset Boulevard*?

Convinced that Mr. Blake would love his ideas as well, Charles wrote a lengthy monologue he called "The Return of Norma Desmond," based on her time in prison. (Charles had her wearing a sun-suit uniform designed by Edith Head, a ball and chain by Cartier, and Valentino came in to visit and dance the tango with Norma in the prison yard.)

But when Charles presented the skit idea to Arthur Blake, it was deemed too long, and Mr. Blake said it was "not quite right" for his act. So Charles decided to develop it for himself, along with a few lines for Eleanor Roosevelt ("**The economy fluctuates. Sometimes it flucts up, sometimes down**" or "**I've just returned from Mexico. ¡Olé! ¡Olé! ANY old lay!**").

He created the Bette Davis routine about birthing babies, and the Yankees coming to burn Atlanta and rape all the women. After he did some of this material at a party the following week, the owners of Club La Vie in Altadena asked him to perform it at their club. The response was so good, they knocked out a wall in the nightclub, added a stage, and hired him to perform full time. They paid him $75 a week and gave him dinner (usually a cheeseburger). Charles thought he had finally "made it."

That was 1954. From then on, he remained gainfully employed as a nightclub comedian and writer for another 40 years.

When Harvey Fierstein asked Charles to appear in the 1988 film of his successful Broadway show *Torch Song Trilogy*, Charles was thrilled and honored. He was even more excited when Harvey asked if Charles would write his own material to use in the nightclub scenes where Charles, as the club show's emcee Bertha Venation, would kibitz with the audience between routines by the other "drag divas:" Marsha Dimes, Kitty Litter (not Shelley Werk), and Virginia Hamm (Harvey).

Charles wrote about 20 lines for Harvey to consider, and they filmed them all. These made the final cut of the film:

"**You know the difference between a lady and a slut? Three drinks!** [To a woman down front:] **I see you're on your fourth.**"

"**Have you heard that Santa's gone Country-Western AND gay? Now he's Santa Fe.**" (Rim shot.)

"**I do have a beautiful voice. But look where it's been.**"

"**Oh, it was so cold and rainy out today…**" (prompting the audience to ask "How cold and rainy was it?") "**So cold that a flasher came up to me in the park and *described* himself. And so rainy, even the Catholics were wearing rubbers.**"

Charles claimed to have had more fun on that set than any of the other film and television shoots he had done. He especially loved working with

Harvey, and Matthew Broderick, and Ken Page, and "everyone involved" (he said in interviews) with his nightclub scenes.

He did many press interviews during the filming of *Torch Song Trilogy*. Although the specific broadcast on which he said this is not known, he later mentioned one reporter asking him about his love life. He never liked that question, but this time he finally said publicly that "**Love to me is laughs. My act and a love life don't work together.**"

Humor and comic timing are rare gifts, and Charles got more than his share. He even thought funny. He also had the gift of gab and the ability to find humor in almost any situation, then write about it, either with razor-sharp one-liners, or witty and often surreal longer stories and jokes based on his incisive, insightful observational humor.

And he could ad-lib acutely appropriate, hysterically funny lines.

Those of us lucky enough to have seen him, or better yet work with him, remember his smart, clever material and its resulting hilarity: all that convulsive, contagious laughter that made Charles unique and his audiences appreciative.

It helped seeing him to understand his wit and timing, but reading his routines at least gives insight into the man's acuity and genius. His comedy material needed to be shared, even many years after his reign as the best "drag king," or whatever he was called: Stand-up Comic in a Dress, Master and Mistress of Disguise and Surprise, or **Male Actress**.

: : : : :

In this era of YouTube, it is easy to find snippets of Charles Pierce performances, so you can see him "live" and in person. Some have been posted from grainy old black-and-white videos, and some from his later shows in living, loving color. As mentioned earlier with the actual link address, the Playboy Channel filmed his 1982 encore of "The Legendary Ladies of the Silver Screen" at the Dorothy Chandler Pavilion, a venue which, while more cavernous that his usually intimate nightclubs, gives a definitive representation of his ability to hold a large audience with his comic timing, quick-wittedness, and irrepressible energy.

The show also gives brief backstage looks at Charles's unusual way of changing costumes while continuing his characters' introductory chatter over the off-stage microphone. Posted in pieces and its entirety, the DCP performance is easy to find, along with other Charles Pierce gems. Search "Charles Pierce" (the actor, entertainer, impressionist, impersonator, not the journalist, pastor, or conductor) on YouTube. His "Turban Ladies" sketch from New York's The Ballroom in the late 1980s is particularly entertaining, and is almost verbatim as printed here in Chapter 2.

One particularly typical video of Charles on stage is a YouTube posting of "Charles Pierce and Dame Edna," where Charles gets the first eight-and-a-half minutes of the 11-minute piece, with highlights of his Bette Davis at the Chandler, then a quick change and his two closing songs, "Illusions" and "One Of The Boys." Dame Edna gets only the last few minutes, doing a song called "What My Public Means To Me."

(Charles DID admire Barry Humphries, the man behind Dame Edna, especially when Barry so simply and brilliantly summarized what he and Charles did: "The duty of an actor," Barry said, "is to be able to impersonate anything: a child, an old man, a tree, a chair, a woman.")

Another Charles Pierce posting on YouTube from YesterGayTV starts with a couple minutes of stereotypical '70s drag performers, then several colorful moments from Charles's shows, and a rare interview with Charles at home, going through his costume closet.

After watching several YouTube postings on a specific topic, there are usually examples of similar ones "you might also like." In viewing some of them, it is fascinating to see how much of Charles's material other entertainers have borrowed, or used verbatim. As far as I know, all the material used in this book was original to or by Charles (or purchased by him). Any use of it by other performers, while inevitable and even expected, should rightly be credited to Charles for originating it, even if other writers had sold material to him for his show. Call it an "homage" to give credit where it is due.

In 1987, Charles and a film production group called Cocktail Video did a videotaped evening at The Ballroom in New York. Lucille Ball and Harvey Fierstein are in the audience, and the production includes several of Charles's ladies arriving at the show: Barbara Stanwyck and Joan Collins among them, to watch Charles's show featuring Ms. Stanwyck and Ms. Collins, along with his other usual impressions.

There are also two rare 33-rpm phonograph records in existence. The first, called "For Pierce'd Ears," featured Charles's early comedy material from the '50s and '60s. The other was the Blue Thumb Records' "Les Natali presents CHARLES PIERCE Recorded Live at Bimbo's, San Francisco," spliced together from several shows he did there in 1975.

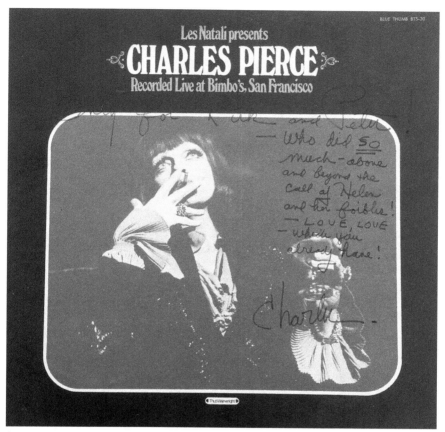

Cover of the record album from his shows at Bimbo's in 1975, inscribed by Charles: "Only for Kirk and Peter – who did <u>so</u> much – above and beyond the call of Helen [from *Geese*] and her foibles! – LOVE, LOVE – which you already have! Charles."

If you weren't fortunate enough to have witnessed Charles live on stage, you would do yourself a favor to watch / listen to any of Charles's live performances on old vinyl recordings, VHS tapes, DVDs, or the many YouTube postings. All of the writing about his funniest material can never do justice to the man himself and his comic timing in performance. Charles Pierce was one of the most accomplished impressionists and gifted comedians of the 20th century, and you really do have to see him to believe, comprehend, and appreciate that fact.

Charles as Bette Davis appreciatively acknowledging a standing ovation. And good reviews.

CHAPTER 8

THE REVIEWS

ritics fell over their words attempting to praise the Charles Pierce comic genius. As compulsive hoarders, Charles and I saved reviews, and in looking back over them, years after his death, I was struck by how positively glowing they were. In fact, of the 200+ copies of reviews I saved or found, there is not one negative comment.

Some critics became friends and avid fans. They would call before a review got printed to share it with Charles (or me when I worked as his publicist), and there often seemed to be a competition. Perhaps they were vying for the cleverest quip or quote which might be excised from a review and used in an ad raving about the show.

James Armstrong, San Francisco correspondent and photographer for New York's ground-breaking *After Dark* entertainment magazine in the 1970s, contacted me after Charles headlined the first of several large-cast extravaganzas that local impresario Les Natali produced at Bimbo's 365 Club. "How about this?" he cooed into the phone: "Charles Pierce is an incandescent urn of comedic genius!" Could it be any gayer, we wondered? *After Dark* was, after all, the gayest magazine of its time. We used the quote. Mr. Armstrong was also an excellent photographer, and took many publicity pictures of Charles, some used in this book (see page 150).

The "straight" media were eagerly as enthusiastic.

Shortly after Charles decamped from San Francisco to North Hollywood in the early '70s, we produced a brochure for his new agent Budd Haas to distribute among concert and nightclub promoters in hopes of getting bookings in Southern California.

It featured about a dozen black and white photos of Charles's various characters. Printing in color was prohibitively expensive at the time, and there were very few promotional color photographs taken of him until well into the 1980s. (He and a greeting card manufacturer created a series of about 40 cards in the late '80s, each with a color photo one of his characters, and funny messages inside. They're now collectors' items.)

The promotional brochure included a long, complete list of his appearances to date, and snippets of critical gush, like those "quote ads" that films and live shows would publish after reviews were printed. The brochure's headline read "**CHARLES PIERCE IS...** followed by:

...**one of the greatest female impersonators in the world.**"
–John Wasserman, *San Francisco Chronicle*

...**campier than the National Guard.**"
–Herb Caen, *San Francisco Chronicle*

...**shapely, elegant, and as 'herself,' the most entertaining element in the show, even including his usual Bette-Tallulah-Mae-Jeanette impressions.**"
–Robert Taylor, *The Hollywood Reporter*

...**a fantastically funny and outrageous man.**"
–Clive Barnes, *The New York Times*

...**a master not only of female impersonation, but at entertainment.**"
–Jim Crockett, *The Marin Independent Journal*

...**the King of Female Impressionists. A dominant performer on any stage.**"
–Barbara Bladen, *San Mateo Times*

...**Maria Callas, Joan Crawford, and Bette Davis rolled into one.**"
–Russell Hartley, *After Dark*

...**exceptional. In drag as Bette Davis or someone, he does stand-up comedy. No singing. No lip-sync. Just someone on stage relying on his own resources, and Pierce is hysterical... priceless.**"
–Sue Cameron, *The Hollywood Reporter*

...**a super camp, a comedian in drag, one of the best stand-up comics we have seen in many a night club.**"
–Lyn Pederson, *L.A. Advocate*

...**certainly one of the greatest female impressionists / comediennes / comedians appearing on any stage anywhere in the world.**"
–*The San Francisco Free Press*

These were all reviews Charles had garnered before 1971. He worked for another 20+ years, and got hundreds more. All gush.

The brochure worked, if not quite as planned. Les Natali saw it and decided to bring Charles back to San Francisco in a "limited engagement" at the opulent Bimbo's in 1971. The short run was sold out, prompting a return engagement at Bimbo's again a month later; it ran six more sold-out weeks. Charles returned in 1975 and the press went wild again:

"There's nothing wrong with showbiz that talent won't cure. By talent I mean Male Actress Charles Pierce who, outrageously gowned, filled Bimbo's wall-to-wall. Charles is an indoor camper, and the best."
–Herb Caen, *San Francisco Chronicle*

"Classically camp, deliriously happy and funny... utterly unbelievable. The Charles Pierce Show is rich, ripe, and grand theatre."
–Philip Elwood, *San Francisco Examiner*

"A phenomenal occurrence! Pierce did all the favorites – Bette Davis, Mae West, Joan Crawford, Katharine Hepburn – and did them brilliantly. It was a virtuoso performance. The place, quite simply, freaked. Frank Sinatra should get such audience response."
–John Wasserman, *San Francisco Chronicle*

The reviews had the desired effect: Charles at Bimbo's became a San Francisco staple in the summer of 1975 and again in 1976, when he delighted in playing along with the country's bicentennial frenzy. Mae West appeared in red, white, and blue. Eileen Gallagher, a local Kate Smith impressionist, sang "God Bless America." Broadway singer Brian Avery performed patriotic songs. Even legendary mime (then a San Francisco celebrity) Robert Shields was in the show.

Charles made pointed references to how far the country had come in 200 years, when a comedian in a dress could pack a 600-seat nightclub during two shows on the Fourth of July, competing with extravagant fireworks displays, which Charles told the crowd were actually in early celebration of his 50th birthday (ten days later, on July 14, 1976).

Charles's mid-'70s "return" to New York (he had last appeared there in 1955) prompted Rex Reed to observe that he "**makes his living putting on two things: dresses and audiences. He's a must-see.**"

The normally tough Clive Barnes raved in his *New York Times* review that "Charles is a drag *king*, not a drag queen, never for one moment pretending to be a woman. His uniqueness as an artist is in the brilliance of his material, with a taste of wit and style to it."

A few months later, Mr. Barnes himself presented Charles with an Obie (off-Broadway "Tony"-like) Award for his Village Gate show.

By 1980, Charles had established himself as one of the most successful cabaret performers in San Francisco, Los Angeles, New York, Las Vegas, and London. He continued perfecting his act, his timing, and his ability to fill a room with adoring fans and raving reviewers for another ten years, performing in Washington DC, Provincetown, Vancouver, Toronto, Portland, Seattle, Dallas, Chicago, Pittsburgh, and Atlanta. The complete Charles Pierce performance chronology is listed on pages 144-145.

After opening night of Charles's third and final engagement at San Francisco's "cross-over" nightclub The City (formerly Cabaret) in 1979, respected performing arts critic for the *San Francisco Examiner*, Philip Elwood, wrote an insightful article under the headline:

Charles Pierce Is Better Than Ever

Charles Pierce, our city's favorite male actress, is also its grandest illusion.

Over the years Pierce has played so many local clubs, cabarets and theaters, that not only do we consider him "ours," we also, I fear, take him for granted – overlooking the fact that he has grown immensely as a performer during the 1970s, and has acquired a fanatical following on the East Coast and in England.

Take it from an old Pierce fan, and one of his sterner critics too – you'll get one of the liveliest, broad and bawdy 90-minute shows of your life. And the cleverest.

Charles Pierce is better than ever.

New York Post reviewer Curt Davis started his 1981 review of Charles's opening at Freddy's Supper Club with:

> **"ILLUSION. Magic. Sleight of hand. Actor. Suspension of belief. Incredulity. Conversion. Faith. Charles Pierce at Freddy's. His performance is one for which all who aspire must see – a combination of comedy, accuracy, and entertainment. Charles Pierce is terrific entertainment."**

Legendary New York columnist Liz Smith was a big fan. In fact when there was talk of Joan Collins bidding on the screen rights to a new book called "Bette and Joan" [Davis and Crawford], Collins wanted to play Crawford. As for Bette, Liz Smith reported, everyone from Joanne Woodward to Carol Burnett to Meryl Streep had been mentioned. Liz Smith's clincher: "My vote goes to Charles Pierce."

Summing up Charles's first of many engagements at San Francisco's Fairmont Hotel Venetian Room on Nob Hill in 1984, Judy Richter of the *San Mateo Times* ended her "Richter Scale" review with "**It's easy to see why Charles Pierce has survived so long. He titillates without shocking. He pokes fun without anger or cruelty. He's a consummate showman and a master comedian.**"

Charles's sold-out, held-over 1985 Mayfair Theatre engagement in Santa Monica inspired Los Angeles critic Viola Hegyi Swisher (previously of *After Dark* magazine) to note that his character impressions were "**not 'imitations.' More than just an impressionist, he's an inspired creative interpreter of famous females.**"

The review on the following page, by *San Francisco Chronicle* staff critic Mick LaSalle, appeared on June 7, 1990, after opening night of Charles's final engagement at the Plush Room. Charles "retired" later that year. This was his favorite rave review, ever.

Again, it may not have been the headline Charles would have chosen, but the very personal essay by LaSalle said it all, and said it better than almost anyone ever had. Or ever could.

Everyman's Female Impersonator

Every time I go to see Charles Pierce, I ask myself if it wasn't just the mood I was in last time. Can he really be as good as I remember? Then he sweeps across the stage, and my doubts go out the window. This is a brilliant performer.

To miss seeing Charles Pierce live is to miss an experience that's unique and delightful. He's back at the Plush Room in a slightly remodeled version of the act he did there in March called "All Talking! All Singing! All Dancing! All Dead!"

The thing about Pierce is not so much that he is a female impersonator as he is a performer who happens to do his performing in a series of sparkling gowns. This is worth mentioning because there are plenty of people out there who aren't all that interested in female impersonation, yet who would love Charles Pierce.

This isn't a gay show, a straight show, a gay show toned down for a straight audience, or a straight show with a certain gay sensibility. This is a wonderful show. For everybody.

Pierce as Tallulah Bankhead enters from the audience in a fur coat, thinking that she is walking into an A.A. meeting. "You mean it's not? Then give me a drink, dahling," he says in her slack-jawed mumble.

Pierce is accompanied by pianist Michael Biagi, who maintains an unobtrusive, steady musical background during the bits. A few times, Pierce told Biagi to "wait for it," as the audience gradually caught the more obscure double entendres. "They didn't let me in heaven," Pierce says as Mae West. "They were afraid I'd eat all the prophets."

Despite the force of his satire, there's something unmistakably loving about a Pierce performance. His generosity extends not only to his audience but to the women he satirizes, and he leaves you with a warm feeling.

Mr. LaSalle summarized Charles's entire comic legacy in that one review. The Charles Pierce comedy was universal, and universally appealing. Author Richard Barsam was an avid and devoted fan, and later became Charles's friend and correspondent. He wisely observed that Charles's humor bordered on the surreal, or as Mick LaSalle noted, was invested with "a depth of absurdity."

Mr. Barsam also pointed out that what made Charles unique was his guiding intelligence, brilliant timing, and quality of delivery that always set him apart from others. It was impossible, he opined, for critics to actually capture the essence of a Charles Pierce performance in words, though some of the ones quoted in this chapter came close.

Charles was that rare showman: smart and funny, loving and generous, clever and masterful. And he did leave audiences with a warm feeling, especially during the HIV/AIDS-stricken 1980s, when laughter was often lacking, yet ultimately became one the decade's most effective drugs. Attending a Charles Pierce show would make audiences forget their troubles, and get happy.

That's what this collection of his comedy material has intended to do: to share it with the world, especially the "CP Virgins." To make you laugh and get happy. And to leave you with a warm feeling.

Charles always did.

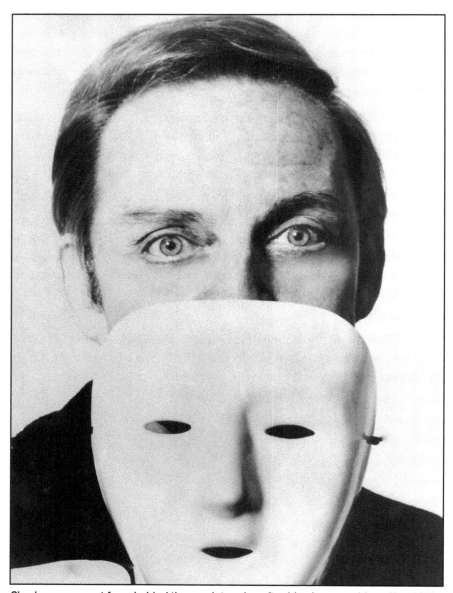

Charles comes out from behind the mask to relax after his show... as himself, c. 1970

CHAPTER 9

AFTER THE SHOW

C harles Pierce worked hard for the money, then loved to spend a *little* of it (remember, he was Scottish) on a post-show martini. His adrenaline was usually overflowing after an hour-and-a-half of non-stop work and, unless he enjoyed a cocktail (or told a few) after his shows, he had difficulty calming down and getting to sleep.

So off he went after almost every show night, although at most clubs where he played, they usually offered him a post-performance drink, and he enjoyed it with his fans out there in the dark, right there at the bar.

There was no bar at San Francisco's Encore Theatre where we worked together in *Geese*, so we would all march off – usually as a party of ten or so – to the very show-biz corner restaurant called Pam-Pam, where the eccentric Yolanda would wait on us, but not before mock-complaining every time about "my nerves!" Pam-Pam was known for its Steak Soup, which made a perfect after-show meal and the ideal way to absorb at least one martini. So when Yolanda came to the table, she would always ask, "Steak Soup, Charlie? And the child's portion martini?" She was such a camp, and she became an auntie to us all.

The first show-biz celebrity to insist on joining us after the show in 1971 was Sir John Gielgud, who bellied up to the bar at Ciro's on the Sunset Strip, and a group of us (also including Martha Raye as I recall) stayed long after the show and put some serious dents in a couple bottles of vodka. Sir John also talked about how well he thought Charles would do in London, which turned out to be quite prescient in 1971. Charles played a successful run at London's elegant Fortune Theatre shortly thereafter, in 1975, and returned to England "by popular demand" for two more engagements at the more intimate Country Cousin in London a couple years later.

After one of Charles's many engagements at Studio One, his fellow Pasadena Playhouse alum Charles Nelson Reilly invited us to dinner at Wolfgang Puck's original Spago restaurant above Sunset Boulevard. At our large round table in the center of the restaurant were also Julie Harris and *The Belle of Amherst's* author William (Bill) Luce, well after the show played on Broadway in 1976, when Ms. Harris had won the Tony Award for her performance. Charles Pierce could barely get in a word during dinner because the other Charles and Julie Harris had their own show-biz "shorthand" and dominated the conversation. This was just fine with everyone, except Charles Pierce. Of course he had much more fun when he was the center of attention.

Throughout the Spago dinner, I noticed Swifty Lazar, famed Hollywood agent, and Fred De Cordova, producer of "The Tonight Show Starring Johnny Carson," seated together at a table just over Charles Pierce's shoulder. They seemed to be talking about Charles; every time I glanced over at them, they were looking directly toward us.

They stopped by our table on their way out of the restaurant, but rather than speak to anyone else, they came over to me, said how good it was to see me, and would I please call Mr. De Cordova's office in the morning. (Oh, and "Hi Charles. Charles. Bill. Julie.") We were all slightly gob-smacked after they left. None of us could imagine who they thought I was, although we were sure that some look-alike Hollywood celebrity probably never again appeared on "The Tonight Show." Messrs. Pierce and Reilly seemed quite offended that they weren't asked, or barely acknowledged. Ms. Harris didn't care. I never called Mr. De Cordova – what would I have said? Charles wished I had.

Almost every night after her two back-to-back performances at Caesars Palace in 1978, Ann-Margret invited the entire cast up to relax in her palatial suite with her and her husband Roger Smith for drinks, snacks, and a movie. Charles got quite chummy with all the performers. Socially, those after-show gatherings were the highlight of his entire Las Vegas experience. He did not enjoy performing nearly as much as he did relaxing after the shows with the affable, appreciative Ann-Margret, and her charming husband. And all those adorable, adoring dancers. The cast seemed to like Charles a whole lot more than the audiences did.

It took Charles almost two hours before every show to put on complete stage makeup. It was an involved process, which he never let anyone watch;

he would keep the door closed or the drapes drawn so that no one could see the transformation from Charles into Celene.

It was also his own personal time to get into character, which actors usually need, in sometimes substantial but always subjective amounts. So it was always amusing to those around him that Charles got out of costume and makeup in just a matter of minutes. His undergarments were tight and restrictive, so those flew off him as soon as he was undressed off-stage, then he slathered on the makeup remover and Celene turned into Charles in about the same time as one of his quick changes. He was usually dressed in his typical after-show casual slacks and sport shirt before any of the audience made its way to his dressing room. Rarely – and only if he was expecting a celebrity to come backstage and have a publicity shot taken with him as one of his characters – would he appear as anyone other than Charles. He was ready for a drink, and even more ready to leave the ladies behind for the night.

Dixie Carter and her husband Hal Holbrook, the renowned actor and Mark Twain impressionist, once brought Richard Chamberlain and his partner to see Charles at the San Francisco Fairmont Hotel's legendary Venetian Room. Charles and the Holbrooks were ardent fans and admirers of each other. After a few post-show cocktails in the dressing suite, our party of about 12 went downstairs to the one of the hotel's late-night restaurants. We ordered a bottle of wine, and about five minutes after we ordered a second, they announced last call. Dixie hid the bottle on the floor between her legs, just after she had slipped off her shoes. She asked Richard to go surreptitiously under the draped table a few minutes later to fill a few wine glasses that she would hand down to him. While he was down there, he hid her shoes under his jacket. He was the first to excuse himself after the check was paid.

None of us will ever forget the sight of classy, elegant Dixie Carter crawling around the floor under and around our large table, in search of her shoes. Even Hal joined in the merriment and laughed with us at Dixie's expense. When she said something that her "Designing Women" character Julia Sugarbaker might have blurted out during a similar situation, Richard finally gave in and called out her name, holding up her shoes for all to see. After a few more choice comments, Dixie joined the hilarity, and we all had a legendary show-biz (shoe-biz?) story to tell our grandchildren. Or our readers.

Charles boasted of the time that Rudolf Nureyev and Margot Fonteyn came to see him at The Gilded Cage, then invited him to attend their performance at the San Francisco Opera House the next night. After the ballet, they all went to a Haight Ashbury pot party, which was loud and late; neighbors complained and the police arrived. Charles found an escape across to the next building, but most of the revelers were hauled off to jail, including Rudi and Margot. The July 12, 1967, *San Francisco Chronicle* reported the "Dancers' Hippie Spree," and that Nureyev and Fonteyn were freed after the "great ballet bust." Charles followed the paddy wagon to the Hall of Justice and watched Rudi camp it up for the cameras, doing his (or perhaps Charles's?) Bette Davis imitation of "What a dump!"

Just after celebrating his 25th anniversary as a stand-up comedian, and the previous 15 or so years in drag, Charles decided that after his regular show at the Plush Room one night, he would appear at a late-night benefit show at San Francisco's glorious old Castro Theatre movie palace, to help retire the campaign debt of Supervisor Harry Britt. It was the 1980 anniversary of the '06 San Francisco earthquake, so Charles thought it would be fun to camp it up for a few minutes as Bette, then lead the audience in a sing-along of Jeanette MacDonald's "San Francisco" at midnight. Also on the bill were David Kelsey at the theatre's mighty pipe organ, and author Armistead Maupin as master of ceremonies. Also scheduled to perform was the newly formed Lesbian Chorus, about 50-strong, making its debut.

Seated as a group in the packed theatre, the chorus seemed surly; clearly they did not enjoy seeing this funny man dressed as a glamorous female, getting laughs by "impersonating" a woman. They seemed particularly perturbed by the **"Liz Taylor has more chins than a Chinese phone book"** line (which was, in fact, borrowed from Joan Rivers).

Charles used one of his old, vaguely vulgar lines from early Gilded Cage days, a joke he had retired once he played more "legit" (or as we called them then, "cross-over") nightclubs. But here he was, in the heart of the gay district of the gayest city, so he blurted out: **"Why do they have a cock on a weather vane? Because it would look like hell to have a cunt up there. The wind would blow through it and give off erroneous weather reports."**

Well, that did it. The lesbians arose *en masse* and stormed out of the theatre, as the mostly male audience heckled them. The crowd made its support of Charles, and its displeasure with the lesbian group, quite vocal.

Charles didn't miss a beat. As Tallulah, he roared that guttural laugh of hers and asked boozily, "**Really, dahlings, am I the only lesbian here with a sense of humor?**"

The remaining audience screamed its approval, and Armistead further defused the situation with his usual aplomb and diplomacy. A local gay newspaper reported the incident shortly thereafter, quoting many of Charles's supportive fans. It also printed a list of the "demands" made by the chorus. Whether they were ever met is uncertain, but it is clear that Charles and his career survived, and the chorus did not.

Charles dubbed it the "**night that political correctness was born**," especially after the lesbians denounced him as racist and sexist.

Charles also got to add another group name (like Pride of Lions or Gaggle of Geese) to his collection. He had once dubbed them a Giggle of Gays. Now there was also a Stomping of Lesbians.

Very few groups disapproved of Charles Pierce. He had coteries of loyal fans – lesbian, gay, straight, bisexual, male, female, transgender, young, old – plus legions of close friends and followers who made repeated visits to his shows, and with whom he would often accept invitations to go out for cocktails afterward, in every city he played.

One of Charles's favorite Los Angeles hangouts was Numbers, a notorious hustler bar and restaurant on Sunset Boulevard at the base of Laurel Canyon. He often took friends there because he was known by the owners and hosts as a regular… a regular diner, that is, not one of the patrons who actually availed himself of the services that the handsome young men were selling.

However, one night after his performance at the "legit" Henry Fonda Theatre, just before Charles's 60th birthday, a handsome young man named Todd came over to our table to tell Charles he had just seen the show, what a great fan he was, and could he please buy Charles an after-dinner drink? Of course Charles invited him to sit down, and it was actually quite sweet to watch the young man weave his spell. We were delighted that Todd was so genuine with his praise. And with his "advances." It was no surprise that Charles invited him back to his hotel room for the night, after Charles made it quite clear that he never paid for such things.

Todd assured him that he was a serious fan. He only wanted to thank Charles for his talent and his performance. He would not be charging for the evening. So they left, seemingly in the glow of budding young love, or at least lust. Charles looked so happy.

He was. He called the next day to say what a delightful time he had with this bright young man, and how sweet it was that they treated each other as gentlemen and equals. But Charles was sad to hear, and report, that Todd was leaving Los Angeles soon for New York, to start a career as an actor and model.

As far as I know, they lost touch. But the happiness on Charles's face that night, and the genuine way Todd made Charles feel will always remain one of the fondest memories of kindness that an adoring fan showed Charles, making such an appropriate and well deserved 60th birthday present for the ebullient, deserving Mr. Pierce.

After years of giving so much to his audiences, it was only fitting that Charles receive such a lovely and genuine gift as his career was winding down, but with his youthfulness still in full bloom. His popularity was as great as it had ever been, yet never before had a fan given back what Charles gave to so many: true happiness, if fleeting, true attention, if temporary, and true joy, however ephemeral.

Ah, show-biz. Ah, life. Ah, Charles. Bravo! Brava!

The End

APPENDIX

My research for this book took me to the New York Public Library of the Performing Arts at Lincoln Center, and to the ONE National Gay & Lesbian Archives at USC in Los Angeles, where boxes of the Charles Pierce Papers are available for viewing. Among his personal papers, I found miscellaneous writings by Charles himself, none of which I had read or known about previously.

Four documents were of particular interest. "Charles Pierce" by Charles Pierce, subtitled "Confessions of a Male Actress," is a short, nine-page typed story of an event in the early '70s that Charles never wanted to talk about: the night a fan shot himself at a nightclub in North Hollywood. It is a story best left untold; Charles would have wanted it that way. My sense is that he wrote about it just to get it off his chest, as it were, and he never meant for it to be published, although he did personally organize all the papers that he submitted to the archives. Because it was such a dark story that Charles never divulged, it is not included here.

Around 1995, a year after he retired, Charles wrote two articles for possible publication in magazines. The better of the two was titled "Is There Life After Drag? or Further Confessions of a Male Actress. Charles Pierce interviews Charles Pierce." It is quite telling, in surprising ways.

The last piece, "**NO TITLE, YET** by Charles Pierce: The Story of My Lives" was his attempt at writing, presumably about 1996, "this combination life story-photo-joke book," which included a brief Foreword (which Charles punned as "Forward") plus eight short chapters about his life through 1969, when he ended his six-year engagement at San Francisco's Gilded Cage. He added one last page with a list of ten other events "to be included" in what he apparently assumed would someday become a full autobiography/memoir.

It did not, but here, published for the first time, are excerpts from Charles Pierce's own writings.

– Kirk Frederick

The following manuscript was written <u>and typed</u> by Charles himself, but was never published. The introductory paragraph below seems to have been written as if the "Interview" were to be published in a gay magazine. It never was. *Further Confessions* refers to his previous *Confessions of a Male Actress*, a short, unpublished piece about a fan's suicide. This is actually a rare and clever self-interview, granting us some unexpectedly new personal revelations about Charles.

•

IS THERE LIFE AFTER DRAG?

or

FURTHER CONFESSIONS OF A MALE ACTRESS

by Charles Pierce
1995

From 1954 to 1994, CHARLES PIERCE entertained night club goers from London to Hawaii. He can be seen acting on "Designing Women," "Wonder Woman," and other television re-runs. He has several videos in stores. He recently turned down an offer to return to show-biz in a play headed for Broadway. He said, "Too much work." He lives by himself in North Hollywood, drives a ten year old car, and has no pets — "Not even a goldfish." For economy sake, <u>(Name of publication)</u> asked him, as long as he talks to himself all the time, if he would put some thoughts down on paper. Here is the result.

<u>CHARLES PIERCE INTERVIEWS CHARLES PIERCE</u>

Charles: When was the last time you were in drag? What show?

Pierce: **No show. I went to Phyllis Diller's Halloween Party in 1994, as Norma Desmond. I went with Bea Arthur and she was also Norma Desmond. We caused quite a stir, I might add.**

Charles: You may. But when was your last performance on a stage?

Pierce: **After I did "Beach Blanket Babylon's" 20th Anniversary show in May of 1994 at the San Francisco Opera House, I headed east in June and appeared in New York at Town Hall with an impersonation show that included Charles Busch, Milton Berle, The "Grand Court of New York," and as their guest, Jose, "Empress" of San Francisco. Also Randy Allen, who did Bette Davis as she looked in later life.**

Charles: You said, "did"?

Pierce: **I said "did." The sadness of it all. Randy died 12 months later. His Bette character was in an Off-Broadway play and he rehearsed right up to the first preview and was unable to go on. The Gods can be cruel. He was replaced by a woman and we know, as good as they might be, no woman can replace a man doing Bette Davis. The show opened and ran four nights.**

Charles: What do you think about the drag performers of today?

Pierce: I don't. There are too many to keep track of. I do not wish to go into the history of drag. There are many books out that will give you all the information you need on the subject. I began my night club career in September of 1954. Yikes, did I really say that? 1954. That was the year Elvis hit mainstream audiences. I hit the stage of a little club in Altadena, California, called "Club La Vie." I worked in a tux with a box of props. A headband for Bette at a dressing room table or one of those pith helmets for Kate Hepburn in "The African Queen." Naturally, I enhanced it with yards of veiling. I was paid the enormous sum of $75 a week AND my evening meal — which consisted of a cheeseburger.

Charles: How are the drag performers of today different than, say, 25 years ago?

Pierce: The drag artists of yesterday were more in "keeping with the situation." I think that's an expression from "A Christmas Carol"?

Charles: Please explain.

Pierce: When I eventually started working in drag I wore gowns in keeping with my characters, and their makeup. "Full face," as we used to say, was never overdone. No huge lips, glitter on the eyelids, or rouge for days. I was an "impersonator," or as I prefer to call it "impressionist," and not a "drag queen," which was a term we all loathed but, unfortunately, has become popular today.

Charles: I hate like hell to keep asking you to explain what you say. But... would you?

Isn't a drag queen an impersonator?

Pierce: Without going into too much depth — I hate depthy interviews — and without too many of those "Well, in my day, etc.," I will tell you this. Up to the late '80s, the performers who worked the clubs and theaters in drag were Lynn Carter, T.C. Jones, Craig Russell, Dame Edna, Divine, Big Jimmy, Fel Andrews, Arthur Blake, and myself. We were never what you call "drag queens." Then, a drag queen was not an entertainer but someone who had a job other than show-biz, who came home from work, got himself up in some outlandish costume or frock, and went sailing off to a party or a drag ball. There is an odd line there, I know, but I will always draw it.

Charles: You had a line in the show about a drag queen, didn't you?

Pierce: (Suddenly turning into Blanche Hudson) "Oh, Jane — how kind of you to ask." I said, "She was so dumb she thought a drag queen was someone of royalty that walked slowly"... then I went into Queen Elizabeth's voice and said, "Over here, Margaret, and put that Cold Stream Guard DOWN. You don't know where he's been!"

Charles: (laughing — a little) Well, I won't ask you to explain THAT. You did have some rather obscure material.

Pierce: Still do. It's all on paper and I have stacks of old jokes. Maybe I will publish "The Gay Joke Book" one of these decades?

Charles: Without going too much "in depth," what would you say was your greatest failing?

Pierce: Trusting a lover. (He thinks) Trusting a lover with my love. That's why I am "living alone and liking it." That was a Sophie Tucker number, and Bette had a song called "Single." Living alone is okay for awhile but it is nice "to have a man around the house." Another song from my era.

Charles: Of course, you're not the only Gay man who lives alone. I agree with you about lovers and the problem with keeping a lover.

Pierce: No. No. I never "kept" anyone. They had to work or the heave-ho.

Charles: I meant simply maintaining a relationship.

Pierce: (He rhapsodizes with gestures) Ahhh, that glorious time when the stranger across the crowded room smiles at you and you feel if you had been hit with lightning. What a jolt! (Does a Bette Davis) The first night together. The first night on the town together. A cozy restaurant with candlelight and wine. Holding hands under the table. Of course, that makes eating and drinking a little difficult, but who cares? You're in love. Then you're promising him trips to London on the Concorde. Off on the Orient Express to Venice, Rome, Cairo. Blah, blah. They either hang on, thinking you are serious, or they know you are not and so you end up brushing your teeth alone. If they do hang in there and keep calling, then suddenly you are plunged into depression and the worry of how to get rid of them. Unto thine own self be true — with a single ticket to Europe. Much cheaper.

Charles: What was your happiest time?

Pierce: That's a tough one. (Looks down at the floor, thinking.) Peaks. That's what I've had. Peaks and perks. And, of course, plenty of valleys.

Charles: I asked about your happiest time on this planet.

Pierce: (He explodes) Oh, for God's sake! I hate interviews. Jack Benny replied to the burglar when he said to Jack, "Your money or your life!" and Jack said, "I'm thinking, I'm thinking." I think, without sounding like a Mama's Boy, I was happiest when I was with my Mother. She was companion, advisor and, let's just say, a wonderful friend. As to when I was happiest doing the shows? There were many, many wonderful engagements. The ones I felt most like I'd "made it" were at the Fairmont Hotels, The Village Gate in New York, Music Center in L.A. and, strangely enough, a supper club on the East Side of Manhattan called Freddy's. I did ten engagements there over a six year period and the thought always crossed what's left of my mind, "Hey, I'm playing the East Side of New York City." Loved it. But, of course, there were many other shows I did that gave me a real perk.

Charles: Like?

Pierce: Too numerous to mention right now. Aren't these interviews limited to space? You know, I have other things to do today.

Charles: Wait. A few more. Please.

Pierce: Keep begging. I love it.

Charles: What is your greatest achievement?

Pierce: **Living as long as I have.**

Charles: Your greatest disappointment in life?

Pierce: **No great film role that could be seen in the year 3000... and those lovers.**

Charles: I think you are better off without them.

Pierce: **So is my bank account.**

Charles: But you said you didn't keep any of them.

Pierce: **Oh, you know... a dinner here, a theatre ticket there. Never the Concorde or the Orient Express. Maybe someday? I'll invite myself. And meet a fellow traveler — with knowing eyes.**

Charles: Do you like women?

Pierce: **I have told you. My Mother was my dearest friend. She died in 1988. Of course I like women. I have a very pleasant relationship with Bea Arthur. We have more laughs than are allotted to most people. I have women friends in every city I played and with whom I correspond all the time. What about the women in my show? I know they said some pretty outrageous things but if I hadn't admired them I certainly couldn't have presented them in such an outrageous manner. And don't ask me to explain all that because I won't. So there.**

Charles: Would you care to tell us more about the drag entertainers of the past?

Pierce: **No, I wouldn't. This interview is becoming tiresome. I don't want to sound like Gore Vidal, but I am bored. (He gets up and starts pouring himself a drink.)**

Charles: May I ask then, what are you drinking?

Pierce: Vodka. Pierre Smirnoff. He's a friend of the night. May I pour you a Pierre?

Charles: No. However, I would like a Diet Coke.

Pierce: You've got it. My friend Larry and I call ourselves "The Vodka Vamps." When I die I want to be cremated and my ashes sifted into an empty vodka bottle and then tossed off the Golden Gate Bridge. And throw in some glitter while you're at it. As Norma Desmond said, "Let's make it gay!" Well, of course, not about my cremation. She was referring to her pet monkey's casket. Aren't you up on the old movies? Do you know what I'm talking about?

Charles: I... I... think so.

Pierce: A Gay man knows all the camp lines in movies from the past. With the writing today there are no lines in films worth picking up on. I think that last one we bothered with was Faye Dunaway shrieking, "No more wire hangers!" in "Mommie Dearest." Sad, sad, sad.

Charles: Do you have any regrets?

Pierce: Nothing like changing the subject abruptly.

Charles: Well, do you?

Pierce: What do you want me to say? I regret never having won an Academy Award. I regret never having been on a Broadway theatre stage. I regret never having sailed down the Nile or made love in a sand dune on Fire Island. Never having found "just the right person?" Look. In a way I have done all those things. That is, in the realm of my world.

I have won many awards for my performances and shows I've been in. Besides the night club engagements around New York, I was at the Beacon Theatre on Broadway for one night in a fabulous show. (Thinking) In fact, it was two nights and we were jam packed. I was with a variety of entertainers, including Sally Rand, in her seventies and still doing the famous fan dance. With The Incomparable Hildegarde at Carnegie Hall. "Frisco Follies" was a group at the time specializing in pantomimes; I came and went as Mistress of Ceremonies, at one point rising from the orchestra pit playing a pipe organ as Norma Desmond! If that show hit Broadway theaters today we would have a run of two or three years. We were way ahead of our time. Even Anita Loos, who wrote "Gentlemen Prefer Blondes" and a lot of films, came on as "The Mystery Lady." It was a camp!

Charles: You have more or less explained the difference between a drag queen and an impersonator, but what is a Male Actress?

Pierce: That was a description I used for myself when I was in a play in San Francisco. I played "Helen" in the two-act "Geese." I was the mother of a gay boy in one act, and the other was about lesbians in the Deep South. It was 1969 and there was nudity for days! Shocking for its time. I didn't use the Male Actress billing for long because other... (he stresses the word:) IMPERSONATORS decided they would rather be Male Actresses, so they stole the title from me. Then it lost its class and value to me.

Charles: Would you care to mention just who were the ones who, shall we say, "borrowed" the Male Actress billing?

Pierce: **I would not. Most of them are doing drag shows in The Big Gay Bar in the sky! (He points upward.)**

Charles: So you think there is life after drag — up there?

Pierce: **In all seriousness and my gut feeling — that's with or without a girdle — I have my doubts about a life hereafter. I think there is something but I am afraid that no one has come up with exactly what it is that we go to. A fade-out and what is that? Oh it would be wonderful to meet up with everyone we've known in some idyllic setting. I clearly do not think the human body developed by itself. But that's another interview, isn't it?**

Charles: For you, has there been a life after drag?

Pierce: **Most certainly. Too much life and too many dinners. I've put on 15 pounds in five years. Jenny Craig, hold everything! I'm coming your way! When I walked off the stage of the Balcony Theatre at the Pasadena Playhouse on October 7th of 1990 — the closing night of my engagement there — I had no idea that would be my last performance with all the "ladies." I had decided to put the show on the shelf for the holidays and start up again in January. However, I got involved in voice-overs for TV and never went back to night clubs. Yes, I have done a few appearances hither and yon that were fun. I appeared with** the Gay Men's Chorus of Los Angeles at Christmastime of 1993 and, as I told you earlier, at the SF Opera House and Town Hall in New York.

Charles: Plain and simple — you have retired.

Pierce: (Raises his hand) Stop! I have abdicated!

Charles: Hmm, cute.

Pierce: You are catching on. That's what Norma Desmond said to Bill Holden in "Sunset Boulevard." Just like that, too.

Charles: So, you did not retire, you abdicated. In other words, you are leaving the dresses, high heels, the wigs and makeup to those following in your wake?

Pierce: You make it sound like I was a boat. Here's a toast to RuPaul, Lypsinka, Charles Busch, and the like. (He raises his glass and drinks.) I won't be here of course. But I would love to know what they'll all be doing with their lives at my age.

Charles: And that is?

Pierce: Can you keep a secret?

Charles: Oh, yes.

Pierce: *So can I. (Gives a Cheshire cat look)*

Charles: You've used that line as a closing for every interview you have given over the last 30 years. Please tell your age.

Pierce: There were two of me on the Ark. I was the one with the beads.

Charles: C'mon. (Pleading)

Pierce: I go way back. I was in charge of gathering up Marie Antoinette's head.

> She wasn't the only queen in history that lost her head over a basket, you know?

Charles: Yes, we know. And no more bad jokes, please. We've heard them all. Your age?

Pierce: I remember breaking a high heel getting off the Mayflower. That Plymouth Rock was a bitch to walk on.

Charles: Stop! Answer the question.

Pierce: My Transylvanian fan club would be too upset. Let's just say I have led a long and...(he pauses)... fruitful life. I have been blessed in knowing some wonderful, fun people. My work in night clubs was not work. It was party time. When I first started in 1954, I couldn't believe I was being paid for having such a good time. That first $75 a week shot up to $250 for my next engagement, and I still felt I was taking money I did not deserve. I was really lucky to have been brought up in the Thirties. I think of that time quite often. I am the last of my family and with so many friends gone, the phone doesn't ring as often as it used to. (Makes a gesture of playing a small violin.)

Charles: A final thought?

Pierce: Jessie, my Mother, said from time to time, "If you are going to live, live pretty." Then she would immediately make plans to have the house redecorated or go out and buy a new dress and hat

Charles: And you?

Pierce: I'll stick with Mother. Live pretty. But, do everything in a moderate way,

from drinking to shopping and sex. Do not blow everything at once. No pun intended. If a true love walks out the door and leaves you flat, sure: get upset, but get over it fast! Who am I, giving this advice? Dear Abby? Enough already. As Bo Peep said to her sheep, "Let's get the flock out of here!"

Charles: I never did get my Diet Coke.

Pierce: (A withering look)

# # #

The manuscript on the following pages, unpublished and undated, was also found in Charles's archives. It was probably started just after the previous "Interview." Charles also wrote it himself, but it was typed for him into a computer. As you will see, these were more like notes toward a book, rather than the draft of a memoir, which illness actually prevented Charles from writing. The text has has been slightly edited where appropriate, but it is all Charles, in his own words.

•

"NO TITLE YET"

by

Charles Pierce

<u>THE STORY OF MY LIVES</u>

"NO TITLE YET" by Charles Pierce • <u>THE STORY OF MY LIVES</u>

"FORWARD"

"You have to be *forward* to get ahead"
–A teacher I once had (in school)

W here are you reading this? In the bedroom, in flight, in an office, on the train, in the powder room? Listen, I am terribly sorry, where and whoever you are, but believe me I agonized for weeks over a title for this combination life story–photo–joke book. It is the story of my life, or perhaps I should say lives, as I am beginning to feel like Dracula looking for a new jugular vein to bite into. Oh, I've been around – and around. More on that later. Decisions! Decisions! Help me make a choice before my publishers cancel my royalty clause. What shall we call the book?…

> "FROM DRAGS TO RICHES"
> "FOR PIERCE'D EARS"
> "CAMPY NIGHTS IN A SMOKE-FILLED ROOM"
> "A MAN FOR ALL DRESSES"
> "THE GRAND IMPOSTOR"
> "THE MALE ACTRESS"
> "OH, NO! NOT CHARLES PIERCE ON MY
>   COFFEE TABLE, BOOK"
> "STAND-UP COMIC IN A DRESS"
> "LADY FOR A NIGHT"
> "IT'S LONELY AT THE TOP BUT IT'S BETTER
>   THAN BEING LONELY AT THE BOTTOM"
> "PIERCE'S ARROWS"
> "PIERCE-ING LAUGHTER"

Which one will it be? Great. I liked that one myself.

Now, let us get on with it.

"NO TITLE YET" by Charles Pierce • <u>THE STORY OF MY LIVES</u>

CHAPTER ONE

"It's always best to start at the beginning"
–Billie Burke in *The Wizard of Oz*

Where to begin? How to begin? Why to begin? I shall begin with… a cup of coffee. I'd love a vodka martini but no, no, no – only after work, and believe me, this is going to be work! It is not going to be easy dredging up the past, as they say "putting things in perspective." So I suppose I should start by telling you my life began many years ago with the ringing of the phone. The result of that call started a long walk down my own Yellow Brick Road of Show Biz.

It was summertime in Watertown, New York, and three days before my sixteenth birthday. "The Rudy Vallee" radio show was on when the phone rang. How or even WHY do I remember that? You see, I don't have Alzheimer's disease, I have Oddtimer's disease – and that is fear of forgetting the punchline. Please do not expect my narrative to be oh, so "in depth" because it can't be. I am not going to relive those "magical moments" of life with a straight face. I firmly believe that I have lived this long by laughing full force at life. I never underestimate the power of life because it has laughed right back in my face on numerous occasions.

Now, the phone call. My high school friend, Alma Judes, was on the other end when I answered. Alma, if my life had chosen differently, would certainly have been one of our lady comics as she had a gift for the gag and could have developed into one helluva foil for Benny, Hope, or Berle. Unfortunately for her, but my good fortune, Alma worked as a chamber maid at the Hotel Woodruff after school. Fortunately for Alma there was a radio station in the hotel and her disposition led her directly to the studio between bed changes. There she became friendly with the announcers – well, she didn't become THAT friendly – but she amused one of the announcers, Bob Mowers, with her chatter and he asked her to be his "script girl" for a kiddie show he was doing for the Avon Theatre on Saturday mornings. Was this Alma's break into the small time? Yes, and she wanted to include me on the show and persuaded "Uncle Bob," as he was called on the "Kiddie's Karnival," to let me read a speech on the broadcast. He did and the rest is not history but it was the beginning of mine.

Alma was on the phone telling me Uncle Bob wanted me to read Patrick Henry's speech "Give Me Liberty of Give Me Death." On a kiddie show? I think that was the first time anyone ever selected material for me to perform – and the last. However, I gave it my all and now for the Happy Ending. Tommy Martin, the station manager, heard the show, called the theatre, asked me to audition, as an announcer's position was available. I did and was hired on the spot. I ran all the way home to burst through the front door and call out, "Mother, I'm a radio announcer and I'm getting twelve dollars a week!"

And with that line, my life began.

"NO TITLE YET" by Charles Pierce • THE STORY OF MY LIVES

CHAPTER TWO

"Daddy always said they can take everything
away from you but your talent."
–Baby Jane Hudson in
What Ever Happened To Baby Jane?

"We haven't had a night like this since Marlene Dietrich opened here," one of the waiters whispered to me as I stood waiting to make my entrance into the fabulous Venetian Room of the Fairmont Hotel in San Francisco. The room was sold out, extra tables and chairs were being brought in from other rooms in the hotel and here am I about to follow in the high heel steps of Marlene, Carol Channing, Ella Fitzgerald, and Tony Bennett, although I doubt if he ever wore high heels. What the Palace Theatre in New York was to the vaudeville acts of yesterday, the Venetian Room was to the entertainers of today – the top place to play. Now it was my turn and I was prepared to go to war with new costumes, orchestrations, and new routines – Mama Rose, aren't you livid with envy? Some of the members of that audience out there are a little envious, too. They cannot believe I made it to Nob Hill. In a way, I can't either. To paraphrase a line from an old radio soap opera, "Can a boy from cow country leave and find happiness in a dress?" He can, if the money is good enough. So here I am thinking these mad thoughts while totally costumed, bewigged, and wearing enough jewelry to choke Mr. Ed, as my mind raced back through time and space and years to the night I made my very first entrance…

MUSIC UP –

SLOW FADE –

DISSOLVE TO –

...a Delivery Room at the Good Samaritan Hospital. The evening is ominous with rolls of thunder and flashes of lightning, highlighting "The City of Trees," Watertown, New York. The year was 1926. The date is July 14th. The time is 9:15 p.m. Clouds part like curtains and disgorge pain and hail. Everything has been timed for my entrance. Father's pacing. Mother's shrieking, the doctor is hovering, and finally... here comes Charles! For my first appearance I wore a caul, a membrane mask that covered my face. Was this to signify what was to come later in my life, a desire to dress up and disguise myself?

The doctor deftly removed this "fetal membrane" from my wee head, I took a deep breath, Father stopped pacing, Mother calmed down, Nurse Alma pointed and said, "This – is a BOY!" Then my Grandfather, the doctor, packed up his instruments and went home in the rain, thunder, and lightning and said to my Grandmother, "Elizabeth, we have a Grandson."

So, I was named after my Grandfather, Charles Edwin Pierce, who upon making this announcement to my Grandmother, got back in his car, drove to a fishing shack on the St. Lawrence river and proceeded to get smashed.

"NO TITLE YET" by Charles Pierce • <u>THE STORY OF MY LIVES</u>

CHAPTER THREE

"Okay, fellows, knock it off!"
–Marie Antoinette

As everyone seems to know, July 14th is Bastille Day. If someone asks my birthdate and I say "July 14th," immediately it's, "Oh, Bastille Day!" I know there was a lot of storming of walls, but were they the good guys or the bad guys? I hate to think that Marie Antoinette and Louis had to give up all their lavish palaces and parties and clothes. After all, weren't they only "living pretty"?

In 1926, Calvin Coolidge was president, motion picture sound was introduced at the Philadelphia World's Fair, and Rudolph Valentino had danced his last tango. Poor Rudy.

Gerald and Jessie Pierce were my parents, a damned good looking couple who were the epitome of the Roaring Twenties. Mother, with her bobbed hair and Charleston dresses, and Dad in his white flannels and yachting blazer were the life of every party they attended.

Baby Charles went to live with them in their little bungalow on Pleasant Street. Mother was the housewife and Dad was the breadwinner. Those were the roles they played their entire lives. The Pleasant home was always called "Jessie's Doll House" because as sparse as money was, she somehow managed to have the place look like something out of House and Garden.

Father was a traveling grocery salesman, a breed of men that died out when supermarkets took over. He loved his job, which took him to towns around Watertown in upstate New York, towns with names like Barnes Corners, Adams Center, and Evans Mills. In the summer when the St. Lawrence River was free of ice, he would travel by motor boat to Grindstone Island where one of his customers had the small store. I went with him several times, and learned the peace, quiet, and solitude of Grindstone in the mid-'30s.

My Father drove in all kinds of weather to grocery stores in need of supplies. He worked from 7:00 in the morning till dinnertime, six days a week. Dad had chronic asthma and a glass eye, and worked for $27 a week! He worked for his Uncle Seely who made Scrooge look like Glinda the Good. The office resembled a counting house in a Dickens novel, with its oily floors, decrepit desks, and clerks hovering over their ledgers. Dad brought in over a thousand dollars a week, even in the height of the Great Depression. Uncle Seely gave him a miserly $200 Christmas bonus with a reminder to be at work at 7 a.m. New Year's Day to take the annual inventory. When Uncle Seely called and Mother answered the phone, he would always say "Girl, is boy there?" She put up with this insult as long as she could, and one day finally said "Seely, if you're calling Tarzan and Jane, they're in Africa!"

When Uncle Seely died, he left the business to his wife who, when she died, left it to Seely's mother. When she cashed in her chips, and there were plenty, every member of the family got $5,000 each, which was a lot of cash in the '40s. But the five salesmen who did all the ground work for the business each got nothing.

Dad went to work for another distributor with a guarantee and a percentage. At last, a chance after so many years to make some good money. Not so. His percentage was so high, the owners became distraught that he was making almost as much as they were, so they dropped him back to straight salary. He went on playing "Willy Loman" the rest of his life.

When his asthma got worse and his good eye was acting up, Mother took over driving to the grocery stores so he could take down orders for supplies. She drove him for three years, besides keeping up her household duties. Then after driving through a terrible snowstorm one winter, she finally said, "Gerald, I just can't do it any more." He hated to end his life on the road, but it was finally "so long customers" and "hello office work."

He was still working behind a desk at 73, when a bout with asthma sent him to the hospital where the doctors decided to scope his lungs to see "just what IS causing all this congestion"? The totally unnecessary operation brought on a stroke and Dad was gone within a week.

Death of an unrewarded salesman.

**Charles & his mother Jessie
in a Watertown newspaper clipping,
1932**

CHAPTER FOUR

> **"By the way, there is a name for you ladies but it**
> **isn't used in High Society – outside of a kennel!"**
> –Joan Crawford in *The Women*

My Mother Jessie had a slightly bitchy sense of humor and she used it to do impressions of her relatives and some of the "locals." She did these behind their backs and once it got her in trouble. And I helped. I loved my Grandmother Pierce, Dad's Mother, but she had NO sense of humor. If Mother did something she disapproved, Grandma's usual line was "Now Jessie, do you think that is absolutely necessary?" Every vowel dragged out. It didn't take Mother long to pick up on that, and of course her imitation of Grandma was flawless.

One day Mother and I were out for a Sunday drive with my Grandparents when I, then ten years old, spoke up and said, "Mother, do your impression of Grandma."

Mother's face turned as red as her lipstick. "Why Charles, I don't know what you're talking about."

"Oh yes you do," then I proceeded to do my impression of Grandma, which was actually an impression of Mother's.

Maybe at that tender age I thought everyone was supposed to do impressions, so I addressed my Grandfather who was driving. "Now Charlie," I said, dragging out every vowel, "do you think taking this bumpy back road is absolutely necessary?"

Grandpa smiled and said, "That does sound like you Elizabeth."

Grandma, like Queen Victoria, was "not amused." "Well!," she said, "If I sound like that you won't hear a peep out of me the rest of the day." Then, wonder of wonders, she actually chuckled. "You know, Charles, I believe I DO sound like that. Even as a young girl I sounded like that."

Mother, who was cringing in the back seat, said, "I don't know where Charles ever got the idea I could do your voice, Mother. He has been seeing too many movies lately, and doing his own impressions of the stars."

Jessie was the youngest of the four daughters of Annie and Archibald Hickman. Her sisters, my aunts, were Margaret, Lulu, and Nellie. Mother was always "Babe" for obvious reasons. They were all born exactly two years apart. Grandpa Hickman arrived in Canada in the early 1900s from his home in Edinburgh, Scotland. He was a paper maker so that was the work he sought in the "new country."

His first daughter Margaret had just been born, but the call of the wild (or the vast lumber fields around Quebec) was too great, so Annie and Maggie were left waving from the dock as he sailed away to new paper mills in Canada.

"Hoot Mon," as he was sometimes called, entertained the other passengers on the voyage by playing his accordion and telling funny stories, a forerunner of the stand-up comic with a gimmick. If this had been an MGM musical, Grandpa would have been "discovered" by a fellow traveler/entrepreneur who was on his way to New York City "to open a restaurant with entertainment; so Hoot Mon, why don't you come along and join me?"

Well, that only happened in the movies, so Archie settled outside Quebec and found a job making paper. Soon he sent for Annie and Maggie, who were probably still waving on the dock in Edinburgh.

CHAPTER FIVE

"You have to fight and claw and scratch for everything you want. Do you understand? For EVERYTHING!"
–Barbara Stanwyck, in every film she was ever in

I was thirteen, in the library of my school, South Junior High, playing gym hooky. I would do ANYTHING to get out of gym. I hated the locker room. I also hated taking a shower and worse, I was always the last to be chosen when teams were formed. Gym just wasn't for me – ever. Mother would write notes, "Please excuse Charles, etc…" I forged a note or two myself. So while my fellow classmates were knocking themselves out improving their bodies, I was in the library trying to improve my mind. That meant reading Theater Arts magazine. I devoured any article written about theater or movies. The entire text of a popular play was reprinted in the back of the magazine, which took care of a study period right there.

Then one day I saw it! An ad for the Pasadena Playhouse, showing acting students in makeup class, in dance class, and lounging in the California sun, reading their scripts. Imaginary trumpets sounded, an orchestra played a fanfare – "THIS IS FOR ME!" I sent for the catalogue, which really showed me what I was missing – fame! fun! fortune! California here I come!

Naturally a thirteen year old couldn't take off for the Land of Fantasy, so I waited and contented myself with going to the movies, listening to the radio, and acting in school plays. I even played a rather woebegone pilgrim – emphasis on the grim – looking like something the Indians dragged OUT. I had one line in the school play, "I bring you all a basket of corn." Corn? Another foreboding of things to come in my career?

"NO TITLE YET" by Charles Pierce • <u>THE STORY OF MY LIVES</u>

CHAPTER SIX

"My God! I look like ten pounds of pot roast!"
–Ethel Merman to herself in my dressing room mirror

Jimmy Donohue's claim to fame was fleeting but fun. He was the cousin of Barbara Hutton, the Woolworth heiress. He was a playboy, insatiable when it came to night-clubbing. He never worked a day in his life. "The luck of the Irish," he used to say. I told Jimmy that the very first Woolworth store opened in Watertown, New York; it was a five-and-ten-cent store. He probably had the first dime I ever made! I used to go into Woolworth's and buy a dime box of artificial nails, then go home and glue them on, pretending I was Fu Man Chu.

Jimmy was devoted to my show, and no matter what I was doing on stage, he and his entourage would arrive at the club, often completely disrupting the show, but delighting the owners because the group meant big bucks in the till. Of course if I was doing "live" material, I would talk them to their table, making jokes about Jimmy until they all got settled. Then I would go on with the show.

Jimmy was always surrounded by leeches, lovers, and friends who enjoyed his company AND his money. His bar tab in one night could run as high as $400, and in 1956 Miami, that was a lot of drinks.

He was also "involved" with the Duke and Duchess of Windsor who, I'm sure, looked on Jimmy as a court jester rather than a sex object, as was rumored. His rowdy ways eventually turned them off and they ignored him, which didn't faze Jimmy in the least.

One night at Club Echo, when he and his friends were hell-raising, Jimmy appeared backstage, slipped money in my hand, and said, "Put me in drag and let me walk on stage. I'll show them a thing or two."

He had slipped a hundred-dollar bill in my hand, a sizable sum in those days. While my performing partner Rio Dante was on stage doing "a single," I slapped some makeup on Jimmy, found a blonde wig, and put him in a God-awful thrift shop dress. He looked like the famous movie star Marion Davies. Rio came off stage, saw Jimmy, went into shock and then hysterics – the giggling kind.

In those days, we didn't have recording tapes. We worked right off LPs or 78s. I found an album with showgirl music, dropped it onto the photograph turntable, opened the curtains, and Jimmy paraded out for his friends and the audience, which was stunned. Then I lowered the Jeanette MacDonald swing draped in flowers and lights. Having seen my show before, Jimmy took his cue and got on the swing, then proceeded to soar out over the audience, having a gay old time. By then everyone caught on and they all entered the spirit, clapping and laughing until – the swing broke!

Jimmy hit the front table like "a meadow muffin from a tall cow's ass," as I have been known to say in the show. Glasses and bottles flew every which way like crystal birds in flight. It wasn't that Jimmy was a big man, he was just heavy and when he hit that table, you heard it. I think the vibration sent the photograph needle across the record, but undaunted, Jimmy climbed back on stage, rearranged his boobs, set his wig right, and left the stage blowing kisses to all. If Andy Warhol was right about everyone's 15 minutes of fame, Jimmy was a star for about 10. That was long enough, thank you.

Poor, fun-loving Jimmy. Several years later he was found dead in bed, having taken too many sleeping pills after a night of booze and boys. As I love to twist words, I suggested Jimmy's tombstone read, "He did it the SOFT way." It was Bette Davis who wanted "She did it the HARD way" on her tombstone.

Well, it was a thought.

CHAPTER SEVEN

"I don't want to talk to any woman whose voice is lower than mine."
–Welton Smith, after stumbling out of a lesbian bar.

I opened on Miami Beach at the Echo Club [aka Club Echo] on Collins Avenue in December of 1954. My act was "live" – no pantomimes to recordings just yet. I wore a tuxedo and dragged out feather boas, hats, wigs, and props from a box on the piano. I got $225 a week, good money in "those days." I was on the bill with Doodles and Spider, a crazy record act who had made it into the 'Big Time' by opening for Judy Garland at The Palace in New York.

The bar of the Echo Club was to the right of the stage and very close. Anyone sitting on a stool down front would practically be in the show. Every night of the first two weeks I was doing my act, I couldn't help notice a slim, elegantly dressed man sitting cross-legged, arm on the bar, with a cigarette in a holder, and laughing at the same jokes he had heard the previous nights. Anyone with this air of sophistication should have been sipping a martini or glass of champagne. This man was holding a bottle of beer. Finally, I couldn't stand it any longer and between shows I sat down next to him and ordered a 7-Up, the strongest thing I drank then.

He said, "Do you smell owl feathers burning?"

What does one say to that? I did say, "That's the damnedest pick-up line I've ever heard."

He laughed and gave me his card. It said only "Rio."

"I'm Rio, just Rio. I'm not from Rio. I am Rio."

I thought maybe I should flee backstage NOW to repair my makeup, but he went on. "I've been enjoying your show every night for the past two weeks. I appreciate it because you don't stick strictly to a script. We 'regulars' like that. Your ad-libbing with the customers from the stage is great!"

So, I was being complimented and I stayed, forgetting about my makeup repair job. Rio continued coming to the Echo almost every night during that season and by the time I left in the spring of '55 we had become good friends. I was sorry to say good-bye but other engagements were pending up north. I left Miami Beach wondering if I would ever return.

I went on to an engagement in New York City at Jimmy Kelly's Heaven, a room so small we didn't need a microphone. (How small was it? You had to go outside to change your mind. Even the mice were stooped. Old lines are best.) I worked with Junior Morrow who sang parodies and talked about her poodles Can-Can and Bon-Bon. She introduced me to the makeup base I use to this day. Junior's real name was Helen Myers. Loved her and her sense of humor; she used to paint the Statue of Liberty on the heads of pins and sell them outside her Greenwich Village apartment.

Three months after leaving the Echo Club I got a call from Rio who said "Brownie (the owner) wants you back here for the season, and guess what? I am going to play for you!" I knew Rio played piano but had no idea he wanted to "get into the business." I agreed.

I knew I couldn't open again without something new for the Miami "regulars" who came in night after night. A friend in New York had some Charleston dresses in his closet. Yes, I said HIS closet. He gave me the dresses and assorted '20s hats, furs, and beads, which became the basis for some pantomime numbers I did from *The Boy Friend*, playing on Broadway at the time. The cast album had just been released. I gave notice at Jimmy Kelly's, which I think was ready to fold anyway, bought a Statue of Liberty pin from Junior Morrow, kissed the lover I'd been living with for five months, and caught a plane for the return to Miami Beach and a reunion with Rio, who eventually became known as Rio Dante.

The great impressionist Arthur Blake once described Rio as "The Martita Hunt of the Twilight Zone." (Martita Hunt was a distinguished

British actress memorably known for her role as Miss Havisham in the film of *Great Expectations*. She was also seen as Helen Hayes's Lady-in-Waiting in *Anastasia*. She was famous for her long nose and aristocratic manner.) Yet, in the fifteen years Rio and I worked together preforming hundreds of skits and record pantomimes, not once did we think of a number for Rio to do as Miss Havisham.

Instead he always played Dracula, the voice of Elaine May [in pantomimes to Nichols and May comedy routines from the '50s and '60s], Ethel Merman, or The Bird Lady from *Mary Poppins*. He did "Climb Every Mountain" as a Nun who lifted her robe at the end of the "serious" number and roller-skated off stage.

Rio and I were the first to dare doing a parody of nuns in a show, and we were the first to use stereophonic sound for our pantomimes. We were also the first to "splice" numbers together; reel-to-reel tape recorders became popular in the late '50s, and we were able to create routines dubbing other records. For example, Rio, dressed in a long, flowing cloak and turban, pantomimed Julie Andrews's voice to "I Could Have Danced All Night." On another record, I found a funny "bleep" sound, which I used in place of "Danced" or other places like "I could have spread my wings." "Wings" went out and I put in a bleep. This went on for the entire number, with Rio making appropriate facial expressions at each bleep, to hysterical effect, which we would not have gotten had he done the number "straight."

Another example: I think this was probably the most obscure number Rio ever did. He mouthed Frank Sinatra's "All The Way" as a fakir singing to a wicker basket with a rubber snake inside, attached to a string up over a ceiling rafter. Dressed this time like a reject from any Maria Montez film, Rio mouthed the words, urging the snake out; I was backstage pulling on the string, making its head pop up then go back during the entire number. On the last note, I gave the string a tug, sending the thing up into the rafters. There was a little card tied to the snake's tail, and as it disappeared, the audience could read "Fuck You." Racy for Miami Beach – "in those days!"

Just after Rio died in 1989, I sifted through my file of his letters to me over the years. There was one that caught my eye, and I re-read it only to realize just how clever the man was with words, or else he spent a lot of time going through his dictionary. The letter was dated September 20, 1980, sent to thank me for a gift I had sent him from the Thousand Islands on the St. Lawrence River. The gift was an ashtray in the shape of Boldt Castle, a tourist attraction on the river. Every year on my visit there with Mother, I would send him a card with a picture of the castle, but this year I sent the tackiest of all possible ashtrays instead, and this was his response:

"Never have I received such an Awful, Beastly, Crapulent, Dreadful, Excretory, Flatulent, Ghastly, Horrid, Indecent, Jaundiced, Klutzy (sorry), Loathsome, Miserable, Noxious, Odious, Pitiful, Quirky, Repellent, Sorry, Tawdry, Underhanded, Vicious, Wretched, Xenogamous, Yukky, Zilch excuse for a gift."

CHAPTER EIGHT

"Life is like a toilet seat. It has its ups and downs."
–Don Kobus, who sells lavatories to the jets

How I ever made it through the first ten years of my life I leave to my Mother and Grandpa Pierce. They nursed me through all the childhood diseases. I had scarlet fever, mumps, chicken pox, flu, colds, cramps (some faked so I could stay home from school), acne, eczema and asthma – the worst! Grandpa, as a doctor, prescribed something called "Asthmador" cigarettes for me to smoke: horrible, medicinal tobacco to bring up congested phlegm from my lungs. What a way to go! Is it any wonder I had no desire to smoke when I could?

When I did Bette Davis I'd "inhale" but hold the smoke in my mouth (not into my lungs), then exhale. After playing smoke-filled clubs for years and years, it seemed so odd to hear in later years that "there will be no smoking during Mr. Pierce's performance." When I smoked as Bette, I felt envious vibes from the audience, so I would say "Oh, you people can't smoke, can you? PITY!" (Always got a good laugh.) Then I'd say, "That's the advantage of being a star. You can smoke anywhere you want and they know you in the hospitals." And to someone down front: "Having a nicotine fit?" They would nod vigorously, almost pathetically with pleading eyes, so I condescendingly blew smoke their way. Another good laugh.

During the long run at The Gilded Cage in San Francisco – six years – I got hepatitis. To this day, I have no idea how I got this totally debilitating disease. A pox on your box, Pandora! You can get hepatitis from seafood, especially clams, glasses in a restaurant, spoiled food, uncleanliness, or sex. If urine goes Coca-Cola color and stool turns white, you've got it. And I had it. Fu Man Chu wasn't as yellow.

Yet, instead of a hospital stay, my doctor allowed me to stay at home, eat hard candy and drink milk shakes. That was the cure, so I languished in my apartment administered to by [Gilded Cage performer] Michael de Champagne who came by the apartment at noon to check on me and bring me lunches. Rio came to cook dinners. Other than seeing them, I was alone most of the time, getting my fill of television and sucking on my candies. Ever since, whenever I watch a rerun of "Sea Hunt," or "Alfred Hitchcock Presents," or "The Untouchables," I recall being flat on my back in bed watching them on my rented black and white TV for two long months in 1966.

During that time Rio kept the show going by bringing in local guests, and by "guests" I mean our regular Gilded Cage customers. There were about five who knew the show forward and back, so he let them do the routines they knew. Ray "Sabu" Correia [another Cage performer, technician, and production coordinator] was a contributing factor at this point because he somehow managed to scrape up more costumes and new ideas for numbers. I was gone so long that when I did return, the "regulars" had worked up all new record pantomime skits, and probably hated to see me come back.

It was Easter when I felt strong enough to don a bunny suit and slip into the club unannounced. They were all taking their bows when I hopped down the aisle throwing out chocolate eggs to the audience. Rio, Sabu, and the rest of the cast had no idea who this bunny was, so when I yanked off the bunny head, the place went up for grabs. It was one of my best entrances ever, and a tearful one too.

We kept the show going at the Cage till June 1, 1969. During those years, Art, the owner, sold the place to his ex-wife Pearl, and she made the mistake of using the large showroom six nights a week instead of having performances in the more intimate bar area lounge during the week. In the larger room we were never filled to capacity on week nights. Other factors kept some of our audiences away: drugs were gaining popularity, as were the dance clubs. The times, they were a-changing. Then, Pearl wanted to move show nights to just Thursday through Sunday, and salaries were to move too… down. That did it. I had a conference with Rio and Sabu and we decided that our era was over at The Gilded Cage, and it was time to go.

You can imagine the business on closing night. All the regulars who had seen the show for the six-year run arrived en masse, along with fellow performers from the other night clubs. There were irate customers who had not made reservations, so could not get in. It was an evening of farewell that could never be duplicated, and why, why, why was it not filmed? Video tape hadn't come in then, and I guess with all the closing madness, no one thought to rent a film camera for posterity. I was in such a daze, the only thing I could remember were audience members jumping onto the stage after I did Jeanette MacDonald on the swing, and plucking the flowers off the ropes. Everyone sang "Auld Lang Syne," and Rio, Sabu, and myself cried and laughed at the same time. Now for a rest, I thought. No way.

It took us two days to collect, sort out, throw out, or keep the costumes, props, and assorted items we had used for six years. I remember leaving a five-foot pile of dresses, flats, furniture, props, whatever – in the middle of the showroom floor when we finally left. We took the rest to Sabu's house where he had an empty apartment on the same floor, so we stored everything there. I went to flea markets with the wardrobe, sold most of the stuff, and there were still rooms full of props and costumes. I kept track of all that stuff for years and gradually, dress by dress, wig by wig, I got rid of it.

…and that's all he wrote…

except for the list on the next page:

This final page of his manuscript was a list of the following ten
other events that Charles specifically wrote down to be included
in the rest of his memoir, which he never finished.

TO BE INCLUDED:

The night that Angela Lansbury and S.F. company [of *Mame*] visited
The Gilded Cage.

My first engagement in Altadena; the place was raided on Halloween.

Jay Robinson who played Caligula in *The Robe* – and later went to prison
(for drugs, not his acting) – paved the way for my second engagement in
Florida where I met Rio, starting a 15-year partnership.

Growing up in Watertown, days (and nights) as a radio announcer.
The night I ran away from home, caught the night train to New York City
(I was 17). That was the year a plane flew into the Empire State Building
and they all thought I was on it.

The "Pot Party" raid in San Francisco when Dame Margot Fonteyn and
Rudolf Nureyev were arrested after hiding out on a roof top. I was with
them and escaped down the stairway of an adjoining building.
Herb Caen called me at 7 a.m. to get the scoop on what happened.

The trip to Pasadena Playhouse on the Super Chief – my first train ride
and meeting Ethel Barrymore on board, the first film and Broadway
actress I was to meet [among many].

Studying at the Playhouse, playing small roles, finding out that some of
my favorite Hollywood stars were gay, and being shocked.

The hard times in Hollywood trying to get established as a night club
performer. There were no clubs to play in those days.

Living with my cousins in Tarzana on one dollar a day, and finally
opening at Club La Vie in Altadena for $75 a week.

Life in the '60s in San Francisco, playing six years in the same club with
Rio Dante.

Charles Pierce and Rio Dante, his performing partner at The Gilded Cage, in a *Mame* sketch, 1969

A VOICE FOR THE GAY COMMUNITY

VECTOR was a San Francisco gay magazine published by the Society for Individual Rights (S.I.R.) as a "voice for the gay community." For the December 1973 issue, I wrote an article entitled simply "Charles Pierce!," as a "photo essay" with 16 pictures of Charles both as himself and his many characters, male and female. It addressed the growing acceptance of gays in the early 1970s, and Charles's contribution to it.

Charles Pierce and *VECTOR* have at least one thing in common: they are both "voices for the gay community." While *VECTOR*'s is a voice heard by relatively few members outside this community, Charles Pierce, during his 19 years in show business, has been a voice heard, appreciated, cherished and accepted both within and outside the gay world.

As a matter of fact, Charles Pierce, as an entertainer, has probably done as much for the gay "cause" as has anything or anyone else. He has brought a slice of gay life and gay humor to the straight community in ways that have led to a wider and easier acceptance of gays by straights.

When his six-year engagement at San Francisco's Gilded Cage ended in June 1969, Charles had, in addition to his immense gay following, built up an admittedly underground yet sizeable "cross-over"/straight audience. Indeed, by then, after some 15 years of comedy, impressions, and antics, he had been seen and regaled by multitudes of gay *and* straight members of the press, politics, the business and entertainment fields, including such glitterati as Rudolf Nureyev, Margot Fonteyn, Hermione Gingold, Chita Rivera, Angela Lansbury, Paul Lynde, and Joan Blondell.

Word of Charles's brilliant performances spread rapidly among the "communities": straight, gay, luminary, et. al. By the time Charles left "The Cage," he had become as popular a San Francisco tradition as reading Herb Caen. Perhaps the latter had some effect on the former: Mr. Caen so admires Mr. Pierce that he has mentioned him in his column no less than 50 times in the past ten years.

Charles took a giant leap in bringing his unique entertainment to an even more widely diversified audience when he performed an overwhelmingly successful run at Bimbo's 365 Club in the summer of 1971. The many voices and faces of Charles Pierce were heard and seen by standing-room-only audiences, the majority of which were straight. People who thought that "gay" meant "frivolous," and that female impersonations/impressions were done only by Milton Berle, had their eyes opened and their sides split from laughter. Indeed, they went away from Charles Pierce's performances with a better understanding and greater tolerance of the gay community with whom they had just shared truly unique and fantastically entertaining experience.

Shortly after Bimbo's Charles opened a six-month engagement at Ciro's in Los Angeles. Again, more straights and gays together, more opened eyes, split sides, understanding, tolerance, and acceptance. The "cause" had been advanced another step.

The Bimbo's and Ciro's shows brought a whole new audience into the growing world of Charles Pierce. And glowing reviews from the mainstream media. And more luminaries: John Gielgud, Richard Chamberlain, Diana Rigg, Eugenia Bankhead (Tallulah's sister), Martha Raye, among many who became instant fans.

Currently at Gold Street again, now in his tenth engagement there in three years, Charles Pierce continues to bring together the gay and the straight, the boys and the girls, the long-haired and the short, the young and the old. And the entertainment greats keep coming: Bette Midler and Barry Manilow, the Pointer Sisters, Carol Channing – all new, now life-long fans. And some, like Bette and Carol, life-long friends.

People of every description have left Gold Street night after night with great grins of enjoyment and satisfaction on their faces. They have all become just a little more knowledgable, understanding, open and accepting of the gay world.

Charles Pierce has never considered himself a "spokesman" for the gay community, nor has he ever consciously tried to be one. But in his own unique, entertaining and endearing way, he continues to bring the straight community to a greater acceptance of the gay, and in doing so has unintentionally – but importantly – become a voice *for* the gay community.

At the end of each of his performances, Charles quotes this favorite line from the play *Home*, which he had seen and heard John Gielgud deliver live on Broadway: "If a person can't be what they are, what's the point of being anything at all?"

It summarizes the Charles Pierce philosophy, which contributes immensely to straight audiences' acceptance of gays, as well as gays' further acceptance of themselves.

–Kirk Frederick
San Francisco

CHaRLeS PieRCe
PERFORMANCE CHRONOLOGY • 1942-1994

WWNY Radio, Watertown, New York 1942-43 and '48-'51
  (announcer, organist, and actor in radio dramas)
Pasadena Playhouse Acting School, California '45, graduated '48
Summer Stock, Rhode Island '49-'51
The Broadway, Pasadena '51 (playing a department store Santa)
Balcony Theatre, Pasadena Playhouse '52
  (performing plays and readings)
Cabaret Concert, Hollywood, CA '52
Club La Vie, Altadena, CA '54-'56 (his first paid engagement, '54)
Club Echo (a.k.a. Echo Club), Miami Beach, FL '55, '56
Jimmy Kelly's Heaven, New York City '55
Dimension X, Greenwich Village, NYC '55
Glory Hole Tavern, Central City, CO '56, '62
Ann's 440, San Francisco '56, '57, '60-'62
Onyx Room, Miami '58-'59, '61
Red Carpet, Miami '59-'60
Capri Club, Los Angeles '62-'63
The Gilded Cage, S.F. '63-'69 (6 years, non-stop)
The Fantasy, S.F. '69
Geese, Encore Theatre, S.F. '69-'70
Carol Doda's (formerly Ann's 440), S.F. '70
Queen Mary (the club, not the ship), North Hollywood, CA '70, '72
Jon Dee's Lazy X, North Hollywood '70, '76-'77
Ciro's, Sunset Strip, L.A. '70-'71
Cabaret/After Dark, S.F. '71-'73 (3 engagements)
Gold Street, S.F. '71-'74 (12 engagements)
Bimbo's 365 Club, S.F. '71, '75, '76 (4 engagements)
Magnolia Playhouse, North Hollywood '72
Dorothy Chandler Pavilion, aka "Dottie's Place," Music Center, L.A. '74
  (repeated and filmed in '82)
Applause, California Theatre, S.F. '74
Olympus, S.F. '74 (with *Beach Blanket Babylon*)
Top of the Gate (The Village Gate), NYC '75-'77 (3 engagements)
The Fortune Theatre, London '75
Studio One Backlot, L.A. '76-'81, '85, '87, '89 (16 engagements)
Waay Off Broadway Club, Washington, DC '76
Man's Country, Chicago '76
Ted Hook's OnStage and BackStage, NYC '76, '79-'80
Beacon Theatre, NYC '76
The Office, Sherman Oaks, CA '77

The City (formerly Cabaret), S.F. '77, '78, '79 (6 engagements)
Freddy's Supper Club, NYC '77, '79, '80-'85 (10 engagements)
Garden of Splendor, Vancouver, BC '77
The Cave, Vancouver, BC '78
Magic Garden Cabaret, Atlanta, GA '78
Caesars Palace, Las Vegas '78 (opening act for Ann-Margret)
Country Cousin, London '79-'80 (2 engagements)
Numbers, Atlanta, GA '79
Les Mouches, NYC '79
Grand Finale, NYC '80
The Plush Room, Hotel York, S.F. '80-'84, '86, '90 (10 engagements)
The Ballroom, NYC '80, '84, '86-'88, '90 (8 engagements)
Merola Opera Program Benefit, Club Fugazi, S.F. '81
Pilgrim House, Provincetown, MA '81
Pavilion, The Pines, Fire Island, NY '81
Paramount Theatre, Portland, OR '82
Palm Springs, CA (private club) '82
Cabaret Gold Awards, Bimbo's, S.F. '82
   (winner: "Local Boy Makes Good" award)
The Woods Resort, Guerneville, CA '82, '84, '85
Imperial Room, Royal York Hotel, Toronto '84
Granny's, Dallas, TX '84
Mayfair Theatre, Santa Monica, CA '84, '85
Venetian Room, Fairmont Hotel, S.F. '84-'88 (5 summer engagements)
Mame's, Seattle, WA '85
Majestic Theatre, Dallas, TX '85
Marines Memorial Theatre, S.F. '85
Fairmont Hotel, Dallas, TX '86
Carnegie Hall, NYC '86 (with "The Incomparable Hildegarde")
George's, Chicago '86
Henry Fonda Theatre, Hollywood '86
Davies Symphony Hall, Gay Men's Chorus Benefit, S.F. '87
San Diego Symphony Hall, AIDS Benefit '87
McCallum Theatre, Palm Springs, CA '88
Torch Song Trilogy (appeared as Bertha Venation in the movie) '88
Hotlanta River Expo, Atlanta, GA '89
Tin Pan Alley, San Diego '89
Wilshire-Ebell Theatre, L.A. '90
Balcony Theatre of the Pasadena Playhouse '90
   (July-August; encore September-October)
L.A. Gay Men's Chorus Concerts '91, '93
S.F. Opera House, *Beach Blanket Babylon*'s 20th Anniversary '94
Town Hall, NYC, '94

THE SHOW MUST GO ON.
AND ON. AND ON. OFTEN WITH NEW NAMES.

Partial list of Charles Pierce's show titles over the years:

"The Blondes That Hollywood Forgot"
(various nightclubs, 1970s)

"Legendary Ladies of the Silver Screen"
(Dorothy Chandler Pavilion, Music Center, L.A.)

"The Grand Impostor"
(various venues, 1980s)

"An Intimate Extravaganza with the Master & Mistress of Disguise"
(Marines Memorial Theatre, S.F.)

"Not A Well Woman"
(Hollywood's Henry Fonda Theatre, and San Diego Symphony Hall)

"A Musical Extravaganza Starring the Crazy Ladies and The Living Dolls"
(The Ballroom, N.Y.)

"Fasten Your Seatbelts"
(various venues, 1980s)

"The Last Drag: Charles Pierce's Final San Francisco Nightclub Appearance"
(Venetian Room, S.F., September 1988; the ad used a photo of Charles as Bette Davis smoking a cigarette)
[This was NOT actually his "final" S.F. appearance; he came back to the Plush Room one last time in 1990]

"Legendary Ladies of the Silver Screen, Back Again: All Talking! All Singing! All Dancing! All Dead!"
(his final engagements at the S.F. Plush Room, N.Y. Ballroom, and the Pasadena Playhouse, 1990)

About that last show's name, Steven Winn in his *San Francisco Chronicle* obituary of Charles Pierce said that "even his titles had perfect timing."

ACKNOWLEDGMENTS

This book would not have been written without the encouragement of my loyal and persistent friend **Burt Hixson**, who was an avid fan of Charles's, and whom I met years later when I worked for a cruise line on which Burt sailed. Soon after we met on board in the late-'90s, Burt discovered that I had worked with Charles, and he decided that I had to write a book, "if just to share Charles's funny material with the world." So I finally did write it down, thanks to Burt's insistence.

I also had enthusiastic assistance from my partner **Michael Laughlin**, who read the drafts along the way; he was candid and brutally helpful in his suggestions for editing, clarifying, and redacting, especially when my tendency toward verbosity took over. Special thanks to **Linda Ellerbee**, a good friend whose work inspires me, and whose style I find myself admiring, if not replicating. She was supportive and encouraging throughout the long process of writing this book, my first.

My gratitude also goes to my old friend **Tony Rousos** whom I first met in San Francisco in 1974, early in my association with Charles. Tony helped move and set up Charles's shows in San Francisco and Los Angeles, and became one of Charles's loyal fans. He was invaluable in helping me recall lines and reminding me of memorable stories for the book.

Sincere posthumous thanks to another of my dear friends, the late and great **Lani Ball**, who read the manuscript early on and came up with the title, after I had pondered it for months. "Write that down" was not only a key factor in the continual process of adding to Charles's ever-growing comedy material repertoire, but to my writing it all down years later.

When my enthusiasm for this project waned in its infancy, my good friend and former employee **David Kerstetter** encouraged me to continue and inspired me to keep going, with specific ideas about how.

Thanks also to author **Nick Nolan** for his helpful suggestions and clever insights early in the process. I also appreciate the efforts and encouragement of my long-time friend **Armistead Maupin**, whose writing was always an inspiration. When Peter Still and I worked as stage managers of S.F.'s *Beach Blanket Babylon* in 1975, we hired Armistead to help backstage. Shortly thereafter he came up with the idea for a daily serialized story based in San Francisco called "Tales of the City," which we encouraged him to present to the *San Francisco Chronicle*. It seems to have worked out; in fact, when Chronicle Books decided to publish the first edition of his collected "serials," I spent a week with Armistead at Rock Hudson's Palm Springs home, typing an edited version of the "Tales" into book form. That experience inspired me to do my own typing – and writing – 40 years later. And thanks again, Armi, for writing the appropriately touching Foreword to this book. I am honored.

I owe a very special debt of gratitude to **Richard Barsam**, author of best-selling books on movies and writing about movies, who was a friend and correspondent of Charles's during his final years. I was introduced to Richard through Tony Rousos and our mutual S.F. friend **Art Carter**, then Richard and I started a correspondence and conversations about Charles. His insights and suggestions for this book were invaluable.

Thank you to graphics god **Jaime Flores** for his brilliant designs of the book's covers and chapters, and for guiding me through my relentless insistence on overseeing the internal design and layout process.

There have been many other helpful friends along the way – most alive, some gone. I thank them here alphabetically *en masse*; they know/knew what they did and how, and what it means to me:

Mark, Maty, & Margaux Alsterlind, Artie Anderson, Bea Arthur, Gregg Barnette, Robert Bettencourt, Michael Biagi, Victoria Bloch, Bob Bogard, Kevin Bochynski, Jim Brochu, Dewey Brown, Dave & Cindy Casey, John Castonia, Mary Jo Catlett, Bryan Cooper, Bob Damron, Patricia Davis, James Denton, Dan Detorie, Margot & Harry deWildt, Val Diamond, Charles Duggan, Joan Edgar, Bob Eicholz, David Engel, Rob Eskridge, Wesley Eure, Ken Fallin, Fred Fernandez, Rik Fishel, my sister Kristi Frederick, Steve Fredericks, Robert & Maria Guerin, Hank & Mary Rodgers Guettel, Stephan Hahn, Bob & Joan Hales, Steve Hannegan, Lars Hansen, Bill Harris, Don Hill, Camille Vaughn Lewis Hoffdahl, Roy Huebner, Nick Hyrka, Tom Illgen, Craig Jessup, Arte & Gisela Johnson, Keith Johnson, Pete Johnson, Bill Kaiser, Michael Kearns, John Paul King, John Knight, Donald Lee Kobus, Bill Lanese, Mark Leno, Joseph Lillis, Jenn Lohr, Ed Lortz, Ken Maley, Ron Mandelbaum, Tom Maurer, Sharon McNight, Susan Middleton, Bill Miller, William Miller, Peter Mintun, Lane Moore, Les Natali, Nancy Bleiweiss & Charles Nevil, Frank Nolan, Maria O'Connor, Phil Oesterman, Michael Oliveira, Kile Ozier, Tommy Peel, David Perry, Peter Pierson, Michael Plummer, Tom Quinn, Scott Rankine, Karolyn Raush, Jim Reiter, Rick Roemer, Jae Ross, Donna Rutley, Libbie Schock, Joan Schirle, Jim Schultz, Steve Scott, Kevin Sharber, Robert Shields, Steve & Jo Schuman Silver, Jim Sink, Ann-Margret & Roger Smith, Barry Smith, Phil Stewart, Bob Stickel, David Stiers, Peter Still, Tracy Thornell, Scot van der Horst, John Vidaurri, Lydia Modi Vitale, Laura Voeth, Michael von Behren, Michael von Wittenau, Jan Wahl, Jack Weatherford & Walker Pearce, Tad Webster, Mimi Weisband, Shelley Werk, Stuart Wilson, Steve Wolford, Alton Wright, Luke Yankee, and **Charles Zukow,**
to name just a few....

I also wish to acknowledge Charles's photographers, at least the ones whose names I recall. Most of the photos I have are copies of the originals which had the photographer's name stamped on the back, to be credited; my copies do not. So, except for the *Applause* photos that I took, plus several others that I have credited on the next page, the rest of the publicity photos of Charles were taken by **James Armstrong, Bill Cogan, Kenn Duncan, Jim Farber, Ted Horowitz, Charles E. Iddings, Jr., Susan Middleton, Bob Owen, D. Roberts, Rick Scary, Rocky Schenck, Peter Still,** and **Ed Wassall**. I'm sorry I can't be more specific, but I remember enough to include these names.

Thanks also to Photofest in New York, particularly **Ron Mandelbaum** and **Bill Miller** for their help in tracking CP photos.

Toward the end of the process of assembling material for this book, I was fortunate in gaining access to the ONE National Gay & Lesbian Archives at the USC Libraries in L.A. (thanks to board member **Chris Freeman**), and to the Billy Rose Theatre Collection at the New York Public Library of the Performing Arts, Lincoln Center (thanks to **Richard Barsam**).

Thanks also to **Chris Freeman** (again) of Havenhurst Books for his invaluable help as editor; his suggestions made this a much better book than I ever imagined it could be. I also appreciate **Helen Irwin**'s eagle-eyed proofreading. Publishing partner **Steve Rohr** also offered much-appreciated assistance.

I must also acknowledge, thank, and praise Charles's many pianists, sound, light, and video technicians, costumers, and dressers over the course of his career. His "production coordinators" (dressers) in addition to myself included **Arthur Barclay, Ray ("Sabu") Correia, Herman George, Peter Johnson, Randy Myer, Jack Powell, Tom Roberts, Michael Stanley, Peter Still,** and **Michael Wayne**. Many talented costumers contributed to his wardrobe over the years, among them **Franklin Townsend, Arthur Barclay, Pat Campano, Kristi Frederick, Herman George, Brian Marshall, Peter Morrow,** and, as Charles often credited in show programs, "**O. F. LeRaque**" (think about it: places like Lane Bryant and thrift stores).

Charles's show "techies" were **Ray Correia, Ron Hamill, Michael Johns, Ron Lazar, Dwayne Parks, Shorling Schneider,** and **Archie Webb**. His videographers included **Erick Baze** and **Robert Triptow**. And his brilliantly talented pianists/accompanists were (listed in chronological order) **Rio Dante, Michael Biagi, David Kelsey, Peter Mintun, Don Sheffey, Doug Trantham, Michael Feinstein, Michael Reno, Michael Ashton,** and **Joan Edgar,** plus probably several others along the way. I apologize if I have excluded any unintentionally. The mind is a terrible thing to lose.

Finally, as Charles ad-libbed one night to close the show, and which I did write down, unprompted: "**ALRIGHT! Enough. As Bo Peep said, 'Come on now, we've got to get the flock out of here.'**"

PHOTO CREDITS

Page	Title	Photographer / Credit
iii	CP (Charles Pierce) as Bette Davis	Rocky Schenck
iv	CP as Bette Davis and himself (montage)	Ed Wassall
vii	CP as Celene Kendall	Ed Wassall
x	CP	Bill Cogan
xii	CP	Kenn Duncan
3	*Geese*	Robert Stickel
5	*CP and His Boys*	ONE Archives
11	CP, Bea Arthur, Kirk Frederick	Michael Laughlin
12	CP "generic blonde"	Ed Wassall
15	CP as Eleanor Roosevelt	Bob Owen
16	CP as Bette Davis	ONE Archives
17	CP at Jeanette MacDonald	James Armstrong
19	CP as Marlene Dietrich	Bill Cogan
21	CP as Carol Channing at Gold Street	ONE Archives
22	CP as Maria Montez	James Armstrong
23	CP as Gloria Swanson / Norma Desmond	James Armstrong
27	CP as Celene Kendall	Ed Wassall
28	CP as Mae West	ONE Archives
29	CP as Mae West	ONE Archives
31	CP as Mae West	Jim Farber
35	CP as Mae West	ONE Archives
37	CP "generic blonde"	Ed Wassall
38	CP as Katharine Hepburn	Kenn Duncan
40	CP as Joan Collins	ONE Archives
41	CP as Katharine Hepburn, Plush Room	ONE Archives
46	CP as Bette Davis in *All About Eve*	ONE Archives
50	CP as Joan Crawford	ONE Archives
55	CP as Tallulah Bankhead	Rocky Schenck
57	CP as Bette Davis	ONE Archives
61	Pasadena Playhouse program cover	Kirk Frederick
62	CP as Jeanette MacDonald	James Armstrong.
68	CP, Angela Lansbury, Bea Arthur	ONE Archives
73	CP and Joan Rivers	ONE Archives
77	CP as Bette Davis	ONE Archives
78	CP as Margo Channing in *Applause*	Kirk Frederick
89	CP as Bette on Bimbo's record album	Les Natali
90	CP as Bette Davis	Kenn Duncan
98	CP behind the mask	ONE Archives
127	CP and Jessie Pierce	ONE Archives
141	CP and Rio Dante at The Gilded Cage	Bill Cogan
161	Kirk Frederick	Ray Garcia

index

Abbreviations:
L.A. = Los Angeles, CA
S.F. = San Francisco, CA
NYC = New York City, NY

Page numbers in ***underscored bold italic***
indicate photo or its caption.

See other reference list entries on pages
144-150, not included in the Index.

ABOUT THE AUTHOR

Kirk Frederick was born in San Diego, CA, and lived across the bay in Coronado until age 12, when his family moved to Hawaii. After graduating from Honolulu's Punahou Academy in 1961, then a year in pre-Architecture at the University of Hawaii, he transferred to Santa Clara University, CA, where he majored in English with a minor in Theatre Arts.

After brief stints as a high-school English teacher and a Shakespearean actor, Kirk moved to San Francisco in 1969 where he performed in *Geese*, and later in *Beach Blanket Babylon*. He turned to producing and directing Cameo Productions' *Champagne! in a cardboard cup...* (Bay Area Theatre Critics Circle award for Best Director of the Noël Coward revue in 1980). He also produced the successful *By George!* (a Gershwin revue), and *Beyond the Fringe*. All three shows enjoyed long runs and tours through California.

For over 20 years, Kirk worked as performer, stage manager, dresser and production coordinator for Charles Pierce after they met during the San Francisco run of *Geese*. Kirk also owned and operated his own graphic arts and advertising agency in San Francisco. He often served as Charles's publicist, photographer, and media arts director for newspaper advertisements, posters, flyers, and show programs from 1970 to 1990.

In 1991, Kirk joined the cruise industry where he met his partner Michael Laughlin. They have lived together since 1992 in Studio City, CA. Kirk retired from cruising in 2006, and shortly thereafter began compiling this book, his first.

Lightning Source UK Ltd.
Milton Keynes UK
UKHW040632071122
411784UK00001B/51